MARY STUART

A TRAGEDY

Friedrich von Schiller

(1800)

*Translated by Joseph Mellish
and adapted by Eric Bentley*

APPLAUSE

THEATRE BOOK PUBLISHERS

211 West 71 St. New York, N.Y. 10023

D0167087

MARY STUART

Schiller, Friedrich, 1759-1805.
  Mary Stuart: a tragedy.
  Translation of: Maria Stuart.
  1. Mary, Queen of Scots, 1542 - 1587—Drama. I. Mellish,
Joseph Charles, 1768 - 1823. II. Bentley, Eric 1916 - III. Title.
PT2473.M3M4   1986   823'.6   86-3437

ISBN: 0-936839-00-7

APPLAUSE THEATRE BOOK PUBLISHERS
211 W. 71st St., New York, NY 10023
(212) 595-4735

MARY STUART

"But her marriage with Darnley, his murder by Bothwell at the Kirk of Field, and her too hasty marriage with the murderer, led her subjects to suppose her precognizant of the deed . . . She was obliged to fly from Scotland. She elected . . . to take refuge with Elizabeth whose throne she challenged and endangered. What did she expect? If she looked for romantic generosity she had come to the wrong door. Or did she trust her own sharp wits to fool her rival? From the moment that Mary made herself Elizabeth's captive, the politics of England, and indeed of all Europe, turned on the hinges of her prison door . . . Urged by the Pope, Spain, and the Jesuits, the more extreme English Catholics laid plot after plot to place her on Elizabeth's throne, through assassination, rebellion, and foreign conquest . . . England's final act of defiance to all comers, the execution of Mary, was the volition of the people rather than of their sovereign . . . When the discovery by Walsingham of Babington's plot to murder Elizabeth revealed Mary as acquainted with the design, Mary's prolonged existence raged like a fever in men's blood, for if she survived Elizabeth, either she would become Queen and the work of the Reformation be undone, or else there would be the worst of civil wars . . . The prospect was too near and too dreadful to leave men time to pity a most unhappy woman. Parliament, people and Ministers at length prevailed on Elizabeth to authorize the execution. Her attempt to avoid responsibility for the death warrant by ruining her Secretary Davison was in her worst manner . . ."

Trevelyan's *History of England.*

CHARACTERS

In this English version there are twenty speaking parts— fourteen male, six female. Some degree of "doubling" is possible. The presence of the many non-speaking lords, soldiers, etc., is advantageous but not necessary.

ELIZABETH, *Queen of England*
MARY STUART, *Queen of Scots, a prisoner in England*
ROBERT DUDLEY, *Earl of Leicester*
GEORGE TALBOT, *Earl of Shrewsbury*
WILLIAM CECIL, *Lord Burleigh, Lord High Treasurer*
EARL OF KENT
SIR WILLIAM DAVISON, *Secretary of State*
SIR AMIAS PAULET, *Keeper of Mary*
SIR EDWARD MORTIMER, *his nephew*
COUNT AUBESPINE, *the French Ambassador*
COUNT BELLIÈVRE, *Envoy Extraordinary from France*
O'KELLY, *Mortimer's friend*
SIR ANDREW MELVIL, *Mary's House-Steward*
BURGOYNE, *her physician*
HANNAH KENNEDY, *her nurse*
MARGARET CURL, *her attendant*
Two Women of the Chamber
Officer of the Guard
Page
Non-speaking parts: Sheriff of the County, assistant to Paulet, soldiers, French and English lords, Elizabeth's Servants of State, Mary's servants and attendants

THE TIME: *As the date of Mary Stuart's death is known to be February 8, 1587, it can be deduced from passages in the text that Act V belongs to that day, Acts II, III, and IV to February 7, and Act I to February 6. But Schiller deliberately took many liberties with history. For example, though February 1587 would make Elizabeth fifty-four and Mary forty-four years old, Schiller stated in a letter: "In the play Mary is about 25, Elizabeth at most 30."*

THE PLACE: *London and Fotheringay Castle, which Schiller takes to be in the neighborhood of London, though it was actually some seventy-five miles away. How much poetic license Schiller could take with place is shown in Act III, Scene 1, where Mary sees from Fotheringay to the Scots border!*

ACT I

SCENE 1

A COMMON APARTMENT IN THE CASTLE OF FOTHERINGAY

HANNAH KENNEDY *contending violently with* PAULET, *who is about to break open a closet. His assistant has an iron crow.*

KENNEDY. How now, sir? What fresh outrage have we here?
Back from that cabinet!

PAULET.　　　　　　　　Whence came the jewel?
I know that it was thrown into the garden
From a window. You would suborn the gardener!
In spite of all my caution and my searching,
Still treasures here, still costly gems concealed!
Advancing towards the cabinet.

KENNEDY. Intruder, back! Here lie my lady's secrets.

PAULET. Exactly what I seek.
Drawing forth papers.

KENNEDY.　　　　　　　Mere trifling papers,
The amusements only of an idle pen
To cheat the dreary tedium of a dungeon!
Those writings are in French.

PAULET.　　　　　　　　So much the worse:
That tongue betokens England's enemy.

KENNEDY. Sketches of letters to the Queen of England.

PAULET. I'll be their bearer. Ha! What glitters here?
He touches a secret spring and draws out jewels from a private drawer.
A royal diadem enriched with stones
And studded with the fleur-de-lis of France!
He hands it to his assistant.

Here, take it, sirrah, lay it with the rest.
Exit the assistant.

KENNEDY, *supplicating.* Oh, sir, be merciful, deprive us not
  Of the last jewel that adorns our life!

PAULET. 'Twill be restored to you with scrupulous care.

KENNEDY. Who that beholds these naked walls could say
  That majesty dwelt here? Where is the throne?
  Where the imperial canopy of state?
  With common pewter which the lowliest dame
  Would scorn they furnish forth her homely table.

PAULET. Thus did she treat her spouse at Stirling once
  And pledged the while her paramour in gold!

KENNEDY. Even the mirror's trifling aid withheld.

PAULET. The contemplation of her own vain image
  Incites to hope and prompts to daring deeds.

KENNEDY. Books are denied her to divert her mind.

PAULET. The Bible still is left to mend her heart.

KENNEDY. Even of her very lute she is deprived.

PAULET. Because she tuned it to her wanton airs.

KENNEDY. Is this a fate for her, the gentle born,
  Who in her very cradle was a Queen;
  Who, reared in Catherine's luxurious court,
  Enjoyed the fullness of each earthly pleasure?
  Was it not enough to rob her of her power,
  Must you then envy her its paltry tinsel?

PAULET. These are the things that turn the human heart
  To vanity, which should collect itself
  In penitence. For a lewd, vicious life,
  Want and abasement are the only penance.

KENNEDY. If youthful blood has led her into error,
  With her own heart and God she must account.

PAULET. She shall have judgement where she hath trans-
    gressed.

KENNEDY. Her narrow bonds restrain her from transgression.

PAULET. And yet she found the means to stretch her arm
  And, with the torch of civil war, inflame
  This realm against our Queen (whom God preserve)

And arm assassin bands. Did she not rouse
From out these walls the malefactor Parry
And Babington to the detested crime
Of regicide? And did this iron grate
Prevent her from decoying to her toils
Norfolk himself? Whose head we then saw fall
A sacrifice for her upon the block.
The bloody scaffold bends beneath the weight
Of her new daily victims; and we shall
Not see an end till she herself, of all
The guiltiest, be offered up upon it.
Oh, curses on the day when England took
This Helen to its hospitable arms!

KENNEDY. Did England then receive her hospitably?
Oh, hapless Queen, who, since that day when she
First set foot in England as a suppliant
And from her sister begging sanctuary
Has been condemned, despite the law of nations,
To weep away her youth in prison walls!
And now, when she hath suffered long in prison,
Foully accused and summoned to the bar,
She's forced to plead for honour and for life!

PAULET. She came among us as a murderess,
Chased by her very subjects from a throne
Which she had oft by vilest deeds disgraced.
Sworn against England's welfare came she hither
To call the times of Bloody Mary back,
Betray our church to Romish tyranny
And sell our dear-bought liberties to France.
For, why disdained she to resign her claim
To England's crown and with one single word
Throw wide her prison gates? Because she trusts
To hourly plotting schemes of mischief, hopes
To conquer from her prison all this isle!

KENNEDY. You mock us, sir, and edge your cruelty
With words of bitter scorn. That *she* should form
Such projects! She, who's here immured alive!
Who hath so long no human face beheld,
Save her stern gaoler's unrelenting brows,

Till now of late in your uncourteous nephew
She sees a second keeper and beholds
Fresh bolts and bars around her multiplied!

PAULET. How do I know these bars are not filed through?
Fear scares me from my rest, and in the night
I try the strength of every bolt and test
Each guard's fidelity. I see with fear
The dawning of each morn which may confirm
My apprehensions. Yet, thank God, there's hope
That all my fears will soon be at an end.

KENNEDY. Here comes the Queen.

PAULET.   Christ's image in her hand,
Pride and all worldly lusts within her heart.

SCENE 2

THE SAME

Enter MARY, *veiled, a crucifix in her hand.*
KENNEDY, *hastening towards her.*

O gracious Queen, they tread us underfoot.
Each coming day heaps fresh indignities,
New sufferings on your royal head.

MARY.   Be calm.
Tell what has happened.

KENNEDY.   See, your cabinet
Is forced—your papers and your only treasure——

MARY. Basely indeed they may behave to us
But they cannot debase us. I have learnt
To use myself to many a change in England;
I can support this too. Sir, you have taken
By force what I this very day designed
To have delivered to you. There's a letter
Among these papers for my royal sister
Of England. Pledge me, sir, your word of honour
To give it to Her Majesty's own hands
And not to the deceitful care of Burleigh.

PAULET. I shall consider what is best to do.

MARY. Sir, you shall know its import. In this letter
   I beg a favour, a great favour of her,
   That she herself will give me audience—she
   Whom I have never seen. I have been summoned
   Before a court of men whom I can never
   Acknowledge as my peers. The Queen
   Is of my family, my rank, my sex.
   To her alone—a sister, queen, and woman—
   Can I unlock my heart.

PAULET.   Too oft, my lady,
   Have you entrusted both your fate and honour
   To men less worthy your esteem than these.

MARY. I, in the letter, beg another favour.
   I have in prison missed the Church's comfort,
   The blessing of the sacraments; yet she
   Who robs me of my freedom and my crown,
   Who seeks my very life, can never wish
   To shut the gates of heaven upon my soul.

PAULET. Whenever you wish, the dean shall wait upon you.

MARY, *interrupting him sharply*.
   Talk to me not of deans. I ask the aid
   Of one of my own church—a Catholic priest.

PAULET. That is against the published laws of England.

MARY. I am not England's subject. I have never
   Consented to its laws and will not bow
   Before their cruel and despotic sway.
   I also wish a public notary
   And secretaries to prepare my will.
   My sorrows and my prison's wretchedness
   Prey on my life. My days, I fear, are numbered.
   I would indite my will and make disposal
   Of what belongs to me.

PAULET.   This liberty
   May be allowed to you, for England's queen
   Will not enrich herself by plundering you.

MARY. I have been parted from my faithful women
   And from my servants. Tell me, where are they?

PAULET. All of your servants have been cared for, madam.
Going.

MARY. And will you leave my presence thus again?
Thanks to the vigilance of your hateful spies
I am divided from the world; no voice
Can reach me through these prison walls; my fate
Lies in the hands of those who wish my ruin.
A month of dread suspense is passed already
Since when the forty High Commissioners
Surprised me in this castle and erected,
With most unseemly haste, their dread tribunal.
They forced me, stunned, amazed, and unprepared,
Without an advocate, from memory,
Before their unexampled court, to answer
Their weighty charges artfully arranged.
They came like ghosts; like ghosts they disappeared,
And since that day all mouths are closed to me.
In vain I seek to construe from your looks
Which has prevailed—my cause's innocence
And my friends' zeal or my foes' cursèd counsel.

PAULET. Close your accounts with heaven.

MARY.   From heaven I hope
For mercy, sir; and from my earthly judges
I hope and still expect the strictest justice.

PAULET. Justice, depend upon it, will be done you.

MARY. Is the suit ended, sir?

PAULET.   I cannot tell.

MARY. Am I condemned?

PAULET.   I cannot answer, lady.

MARY. Dispatch is here the fashion. Is it meant
The murderer shall surprise me, like the judges?

PAULET. Still entertain that thought, and he will find you
Better prepared to meet your fate than they did.

MARY, *after a pause.*
Sir, nothing can surprise me which a court,
Inspired by Burleigh's hate and Hatton's zeal,
However unjust, may venture to pronounce.

But I have yet to learn how far the Queen
Will dare in execution of the sentence.

PAULET. What justice hath decreed her fearless hand
Will execute before the assembled world.

SCENE 3

THE SAME

MORTIMER *enters and, without paying attention to the* QUEEN, *addresses* PAULET.

MORTIMER. Uncle, you're sought for.

He retires. The QUEEN *remarks it and turns towards* PAULET, *who is about to follow him.*

MARY.   Sir, one favour more.
If *you* have aught to say to me—from *you*
I can bear much; I reverence your grey hairs
But cannot bear that young man's insolence.
Spare me in future his unmannered rudeness.

PAULET. He is not, truly, one of those poor fools
Who melt before a woman's treacherous tears.
He has seen much—has been to Rheims and Paris
Yet brings us back a loyal English heart.
Exit.

SCENE 4

MARY, KENNEDY

KENNEDY. How dares the ruffian use such language to you?

MARY, *lost in reflection.*
In the fair moments of our former splendour
We lent to flatterers a too willing ear.
It is but just, good Hannah, we should now
Be forced to hear the bitter voice of censure.

KENNEDY. So downcast, so depressed, my dearest lady!

MARY.   I see
The bleeding Darnley's royal shade
Rising in anger from his darksome grave;
And never will he make his peace with me
Until the measure of my woes be full.

KENNEDY. What thoughts are these?

MARY.   You may forget it, Hannah,
But I've a faithful memory. 'Tis this day
Another wretched anniversary
Of that regretted, that unhappy deed—
Which I must celebrate with fast and penance.

KENNEDY. The penitence of many a heavy year,
Of many a suffering, has atoned the deed.

MARY. This long atonèd crime arises fresh
And bleeding from its lightly covered grave.
My husband's restless spirit seeks revenge.
No sacred bell can exorcise, no host
In priestly hands dismiss it to his tomb.

KENNEDY. You did not murder him—'twas done by others.

MARY. But it was known to me; I suffered it
And lured him with my smiles to death's embrace.

KENNEDY. Your youth extenuates your guilt. You were
Of tender years.

MARY.   So tender, yet I drew
This heavy guilt upon my youthful head.

KENNEDY. You were provoked by direst injuries
And by the rude presumption of the man.
Before your eyes he had your favorite singer,
Poor Rizzio, murdered. You did but avenge
With blood the bloody deed——

MARY.   And bloodily,
I fear, too soon 'twill be avenged on me!

KENNEDY. The madness of a frantic love possessed you
And bound you to a terrible seducer,
The wretched Bothwell. That despotic man
With all his philtres and his hellish arts
Inflamed your passions.

MARY.   All the arts he used
  Were man's superior strength and woman's weakness.

KENNEDY. No, no, my Queen. The most pernicious spirits
  Of hell he must have summoned to his aid.
  Your ear no more was open to the voice
  Of decency. Soft female bashfulness
  Deserted you. Those cheeks, which were before
  The seat of virtuous blushing modesty,
  Glowed with the flames of unrestrained desire
  And the flagitious daring of the man
  Overcame your natural coyness. You exposed
  Your shame unblushingly to public gaze.
  You let the murderer, whom the people followed
  With curses through the streets of Edinburgh,
  Before you bear the royal sword of Scotland
  In triumph. You begirt your parliament
  With armèd bands and, by this shameless farce,
  You forced the judges of the land to clear
  The murderer of his guilt, and then, O God——

MARY. I gave my hand in marriage to the murderer.

KENNEDY, *after a pause.*

  I nursed your youth myself. Your heart is framed
  For tender softness; 'tis alive to shame,
  And all your fault is thoughtless levity.
  Since this misdeed, which blackens thus your life,
  You have done nothing ill; your conduct has
  Been pure; myself can witness your amendment;
  Nor are you guilty here. Not England's queen,
  Nor England's Parliament can be your judge.
  Here *might* oppresses you: you may present
  Yourself before this self-created court
  With all the fortitude of innocence.

MARY. A step!

KENNEDY.   'Tis Paulet's nephew. Pray withdraw!

SCENE 5

THE SAME

Enter MORTIMER, *approaching cautiously.*

MORTIMER, *to* KENNEDY.
Step to the door and keep a careful watch.

MARY, *with dignity.*
I charge you, Hannah, go not hence. Remain!

MORTIMER. Fear not, my gracious lady: learn to know me.
He gives her a card. She examines it and starts back astonished.

MARY. Heavens! What is this?

MORTIMER, *to* KENNEDY.   Retire, good Kennedy.
See that my uncle come not unawares.

MARY, *to* KENNEDY, *who hesitates and looks at the* QUEEN *inquiringly.* Go in. Do as he bids you, my good Hannah.
KENNEDY *retires, with signs of wonder.*

SCENE 6

MARY, MORTIMER

MARY. From France? The Cardinal of Guise, my uncle?
She reads.
"Confide in Mortimer, who brings you this.
You have no truer, firmer friend in England."
Looking at him with astonishment.
The nephew of my jailer, whom I thought
My most inveterate enemy?

MORTIMER, *kneeling.*   Oh, pardon,
My gracious liege, for the detested mask,

Yet through such means alone have I the power
To see you and to bring you help and rescue.

MARY. Arise, sir; you astonish me. I cannot
So suddenly emerge from the abyss——

MORTIMER. Our time is brief: each moment I expect
My uncle, whom a hated man attends.
Hear, then, before his terrible commission
Surprises you, how heaven prepares your rescue.

He hesitates.

Allow me of myself to speak.

MARY.   Say on.

MORTIMER. I scarce, my liege, had numbered twenty years,
Brought up in deadliest hate to Papacy,
When, led by irresistible desire
For foreign travel, I resolved to leave
My country and its puritanic faith
Far, far behind me; bent my course through France
On to the plains of far-famed Italy.
'Twas then the time of the great Jubilee
And crowds of palmers filled the public roads.
Each image was adorned with garlands; 'twas
As if all humankind were wandering forth
In pilgrimage towards the heavenly kingdom.
The tide of holy pilgrims bore me on
Into the streets of Rome. What was my wonder,
As the magnificence of stately columns
Rushed on my sight! The vast triumphal arches,
The Colosseum's grandeur, left me speechless!
I had never felt the power of art till now.
The church that reared me hates the charms of sense:
It tolerates no image, it adores
But the unseen, the incorporeal word.
What were my feelings, then, as I approached
The threshold of these churches and within
Heard heavenly music floating in the air
While from the walls and high-wrought roofs there streamed
Crowds of celestial forms in endless train—
When the Most High, Most Glorious, pervaded
My captivated sense in real presence,

And when I saw those great and godlike visions,
The Salutation, the Nativity,
The Holy Mother, and the Trinity's
Descent, the luminous Transfiguration
And last the Pontiff, clad in all the glory
Of his office, bless the people!

MARY. Spread no more
Life's verdant carpet out before my eyes!
Remember I am wretched and a prisoner.

MORTIMER. Full many noble Scots who saw my zeal
Encouraged me, and with the gallant French
They led me to the Cardinal of Guise,
Your princely uncle. What a royal priest!

MARY. You've seen him then, the much loved, honoured man,
Who was the guardian of my tender years!

MORTIMER. That holy man descended from his height,
Taught me true faith, and banished all my doubts.
He showed me that the glimmering light of reason
Serves but to lead us to eternal error;
That what the heart is called on to believe
The eye must see; so I returned, my lady,
Back to the bosom of the holy Church.

MARY. Then of those happy thousands, you are one
Whom he, with his celestial eloquence,
Converted!

MORTIMER. I was sent by him to Rheims,
Where, by the Jesuits' anxious labour, priests
Are trained to preach our holy faith in England.
There, 'mongst the Scots, I found the noble Morgan
And your true Lesley, Ross's learnèd bishop,
Who pass in France their joyless days of exile.
They fortified my faith. As I one day
Roamed through the bishop's dwelling, I was struck
With a fair female portrait; it was full
Of touching, wondrous charms; it moved my soul.
"Well," cried the bishop, "may you linger thus,
For the most beautiful of womankind
Is also matchless in calamity."

MARY *is in great agitation. He pauses.*

MARY. Excellent man! All is not lost, indeed!

MORTIMER. Then he began, with moving eloquence,
To paint the sufferings of your martyrdom.
He proved to me that you alone have right
To reign in England, not this upstart queen,
The base-born fruit of an adulterous bed,
Whom Henry's self rejected as a bastard!

MARY. Oh, this unhappy right! 'Tis this alone
Which is the source of all my sufferings.

MORTIMER. Just at this time the tidings reached my ears
Of your committal to my uncle's care.
It seemed to be a loud decree of fate
That it had chosen me to rescue you.
My friends concur with me; the Cardinal
Instructs me in the subtle task of feigning.
His plan digested, I set out for England.
Ten days ago, I landed. Oh, my Queen,
I saw then, not your picture, but yourself.

He pauses, gazes upon her.

Oh, what a prudent policy in her
To hide you here! For if the youth of England
Beheld their captive queen, through all the isle
They'd rise in mutiny——

MARY.   'Twere well with her
If every Briton saw her with your eyes!

MORTIMER. Never on this threshold can I set my foot
That my poor heart with anguish is not torn,
Not ravished with delight at gazing on you!
Yet fearfully the fatal time draws near.
I can no longer hide my news——

He stops.

MARY.   My sentence?

MORTIMER. It is pronounced. The two-and-forty judges
Have given the verdict: "Guilty." Parliament
Demands the execution of the sentence.
The Queen alone still craftily delays
That she may be constrained to yield but not
From feelings of humanity or mercy.

MARY, *collected.*

    I know their aim: they mean to keep me here
    In everlasting bondage and to bury
    My vengeance with me and my rightful claims.

MORTIMER. They stop not there. As long as you shall live,
    Distrust and fear will haunt the English queen:
    Your death alone can make her throne secure.

MARY. Will she then dare, regardless of the shame,
    Lay my crowned head upon the fatal block?

MORTIMER. Most surely will she dare it, doubt it not.

MARY. And fears she not the dread revenge of France?

MORTIMER. With France she makes an everlasting peace
    And gives to Anjou's Duke her throne and hand.

MARY. Were this a spectacle for British eyes?

MORTIMER. This land, my Queen, has, in these latter days,
    Seen many a royal woman from the throne
    Descend and mount the scaffold. Her own mother
    And Catherine Howard trod this fatal path.
    And was not Lady Grey a crownèd head?

MARY, *after a pause.*

    It is not, sir, the scaffold that I fear:
    I never lift the goblet to my lips
    Without an inward shuddering, lest the draught
    May have been mingled by my sister's love.

MORTIMER. No! Neither open nor disguisèd murder
    Shall ever prevail against you! Fear no more.
    All is prepared. Twelve nobles of the land
    Are my confederates and have pledged to-day,
    Upon the Sacrament, their faith to free you.
    Count Aubespine, the French Ambassador,
    Knows of our plot and offers his assistance.
    'Tis in his palace that we hold our meetings.

MARY. Know you, then, what you risk? Are you not scared
    By Babington and Tichburn's bloody heads
    Set up as warnings upon London Bridge?
    Fly, if there yet be time for you, before
    That crafty spy, Lord Burleigh, track your schemes!

Fly hence! As yet success has never smiled
On Mary Stuart's champions.

MORTIMER.   I'm not scared
By Babington and Tichburn's bloody heads
Set up as warnings upon London Bridge.
Both of them found therein immortal honour!

MARY. It is in vain. Nor force nor guile can save me.
My enemies are watchful, and the power
Is in their hands. It is not Paulet only
And his dependent host; all England guards
My prison gates; Elizabeth's free will
Alone can open them.

MORTIMER.   Expect not that.

MARY. There is a man, too, who could open them.

MORTIMER. Then let me know his name.

MARY.   Lord Leicester.

MORTIMER *starts back in wonder*.   He!
The Earl of Leicester! Your most bloody foe,
The favourite of Elizabeth! Through him——

MARY. If I am to be saved at all, 'twill be
Through him and him alone. Go to him, sir.
Freely confide in him and, as a proof
You come from me, present this paper to him.
She takes a paper from her bosom. MORTIMER *draws back
and hesitates to take it.*

For it contains my portrait. Take it, sir;
I've borne it long about me, but your uncle's
Close watchfulness has cut me off from all
Communication with him. You were sent
By my good angel.
He takes it.

MORTIMER.   Oh, my Queen, explain
This mystery.

MARY.   Lord Leicester will resolve it.
Who comes?

KENNEDY, *entering hastily.*
'Tis Paulet; and he brings with him
A nobleman from court.

MORTIMER. It is Lord Burleigh:
Collect yourself, my Queen, and strive to hear
The news he brings with equanimity.

He retires through a side door, and KENNEDY *follows him.*

SCENE 7

Enter LORD BURLEIGH *and* PAULET.

PAULET, *to* MARY.
You wished to-day assurance of your fate.
My Lord of Burleigh brings it to you now.

BURLEIGH. I come deputed from the court of justice.

MARY. Lord Burleigh lends that court his willing tongue,
Which was already guided by his spirit.

PAULET. You speak as if no stranger to the sentence.

MARY. Lord Burleigh brings it; therefore do I know it.
But to the matter, sir.

BURLEIGH. You have acknowledged
The jurisdiction of the two-and-forty.

MARY. It is enacted by the English laws,
That every one who stands arraigned of crime
Shall plead before a jury of his equals.
Who is my equal in this High Commission?
Kings only are my peers.

BURLEIGH. But yet you heard
The points of accusation, answered them
Before the court——

MARY. 'Tis true. I was deceived
By Hatton's crafty counsel. He advised me
To listen to the points of accusation
And prove their falsehood. This, my lord, I did
From personal respect for the lords' names,
Not their usurpèd charge, which I disclaim.

BURLEIGH. Acknowledge you the court or not, that is
Only a point of mere formality
Which cannot here arrest the course of justice.

You breathe the air of England; you enjoy
The law's protection and its benefits;
You, therefore, are its subject.

MARY.   Sir, I breathe
The air within an English prison's walls;
I am no member of this realm; I am
An independent and a foreign queen.

BURLEIGH. And do you think that the mere name of queen
Can serve you as a charter to foment
This bloody discord? Where would be the state's
Security, if the stern sword of justice
Could not as freely smite the guilty brow
Of the imperial stranger as the beggar's?

MARY. I do not wish to be exempt from judgement,
It is the judges only I disclaim.

BURLEIGH. The judges? How now, madam! Are they then
Base wretches, snatched at hazard from the crowd?
Are they not men who rule a generous people
In liberty and justice, men whose names
I need but mention to dispel each doubt,
Each mean suspicion which is raised against them?
Say, then, could England's sovereign do more
Than, out of all the monarchy, elect
The very noblest and appoint them judges
In this great suit? And were it probable
That party hatred could corrupt *one* heart,
Can forty chosen men unite to speak
A sentence just as passion gives command?

MARY, *after a short pause.*
Oh, how shall I, a weak, untutored woman,
Cope with so subtle, learned an orator?
Yes, truly, were these lords as you describe them,
I must be mute; my cause were lost indeed,
Beyond all hope, if they pronounced me guilty.
But, sir, these men whom you are pleased to praise,
I see performing in the history
Of these dominions very different parts.
I see this high nobility of England
Make statutes and annul them, ratify

A marriage and dissolve it, as the voice
Of power commands. To-day it disinherits
And brands the royal daughters of the realm
With the vile name of bastards and to-morrow
Crowns them as queens and leads them to the throne.
I see them in four reigns, with pliant conscience,
Four times abjure their faith; renounce the Pope
With Henry, yet retain the old belief;
Reform themselves with Edward; hear the Mass
Again with Mary; with Elizabeth,
Who governs now, reform themselves again——

BURLEIGH. You say you are not versed in England's laws.
You seem well read, methinks, in her disasters.

MARY. And these men are my judges?

As LORD BURLEIGH *seems to wish to speak.*

My Lord Treasurer,
I well believe that, not your private ends,
Your sovereign and your country's weal alone
Inspire your counsels and direct your deeds.
Therefore, my noble lord, you should the more
Distrust your heart, should see that you mistake not
The welfare of the government for justice.
I do not doubt, besides yourself, there are
Among my judges many upright men,
But they are Protestants, are eager all
For England's quiet, and they sit in judgement
On me, the Queen of Scotland and the Papist.
It is an ancient saying that the Scots
And English to each other are unjust;
And hence the rightful custom that a Scot
Against an Englishman, or Englishman
Against a Scot, cannot be heard in judgement.
Deep policy oft lies in ancient customs;
My lord, we must respect them. Nature cast
Into the ocean these two fiery nations
Upon this plank, then she divided it
Unequally and bade them fight for it.
No foe oppresses England but the Scot
Becomes his firm ally; no civil war

Inflames the towns of Scotland but the English
Add fuel to the fire. This raging hate
Will never be extinguished till, at last,
One Parliament in concord shall unite them,
One common sceptre rule throughout the isle.

BURLEIGH. And from a Stuart, then, should England hope
This happiness?

MARY.   Yes! Why should I deny it?
Yes, I confess, I cherished the fond hope!
I thought myself the happy instrument
To join in freedom, 'neath the olive's shade,
Two generous realms in lasting happiness!

BURLEIGH. An evil way you took to this good end:
To set the realm on fire and, through the flames
Of civil war, to strive to mount the throne!

MARY. When did I strive at that? Where are your proofs?

BURLEIGH. The great majority of forty voices
Hath found that you have contravened the law
Last year enacted and have now incurred
Its penalty.

Producing the verdict.

MARY.   Upon this statute, then,
My lord, is built the verdict of my judges?

BURLEIGH, *reading.* Last year it was enacted: "If a plot
Henceforth should rise in England, in the name
Or for the benefit of any claimant
To England's crown, that justice should be done
On such pretender, and the guilty party
Be prosecuted unto death." Now, since——

MARY. Can you deny it, sir, that this same statute
Was *made* for my destruction and nought else?

BURLEIGH. It should have acted as a warning to you:
You saw the precipice which yawned before you,
Yet, truly warned, you plunged into the deep.
With Babington, the traitor, and his bands
Of murderous companions, were you leagued.
You knew of all and from your prison led
Their treasonous plottings with a deep-laid plan!

MARY. When did I that, my lord? Let them produce
The documents!

BURLEIGH.   You have already seen them:
They were, before the court, presented to you.

MARY. Mere copies written by another hand.
Show me the proof that I dictated them——

BURLEIGH. Before his execution, Babington
Confessed they were the same which he received.

MARY. Why was he in his lifetime not produced
Before my face? Why was he then despatched
So quickly that he could not be confronted
With her whom he accused?

BURLEIGH.   Besides, my lady,
Your secretaries, Curl and Nau, declare
On oath they are the very selfsame letters
Which, from your lips, they faithfully transcribed.

MARY. And on my menials' testimony, then,
I am condemned! Upon the word of those
Who have betrayed me, *me*, their rightful queen!

BURLEIGH. You said yourself you held the wretched Curl
To be an upright, conscientious man.

MARY. He ever was an honest man but weak
In understanding; his sly comrade Nau
And instruments of torture may have forced him
To write and to declare more than he knew.
He hoped to save himself by this false witness,
And thought it could not injure me—a queen.

BURLEIGH. The oath he swore was free and unconstrained.

MARY. Let them appear against me, face to face,
And there repeat what they have testified!
I heard from Talbot's mouth, my former keeper,
That in this reign a statute had been passed
Which orders that the plaintiff be confronted
With the defendant. Is there such a law?

PAULET. Madam, there is.

MARY.   There is! Well then, my lord,
Why was not Babington confronted with me?
Why not my servants, who are both alive?

BURLEIGH. Be not so hasty, lady. 'Tis not only
 Your plot with Babington——

MARY.   'Tis that alone
 Which arms the law against me; that alone
 From which I'm called upon to clear myself.

BURLEIGH. It has been proved that you have corresponded
 With the Ambassador of Spain, Mendoza——

MARY. Stick to the point, my lord.

BURLEIGH.   —that you have formed
 Conspiracies to overturn the fixed
 Religion of the realm, that you have called
 Into this kingdom foreign powers and roused
 All kings in Europe to a war with England——

MARY. Even suppose it were so: I am kept
 Imprisoned here against all laws of nations.
 I came not into England, sword in hand;
 I came a suppliant. And at the hands
 Of my imperial kinswoman I claimed
 The sacred rights of hospitality
 When power seized upon me and prepared
 To rivet fetters where I hoped protection.
 Say, is my conscience bound, then, to this realm?
 I should but exercise a sacred right,
 Derived from sad necessity, if I
 Roused and incited every state in Europe
 For my protection to unite in arms.
 Murder alone would stain, dishonour me:
 Dishonour me, my lord, but not condemn me,
 Nor subject me to England's courts of law.
 For 'tis not justice but mere violence
 Which is the question between me and England.

BURLEIGH, *significantly.*
 Madam, the dreadful right of power is seldom
 On the prisoner's side.

MARY.   Let her then confess
 That she hath exercised her power alone!
 Let her not borrow from the law the sword
 To rid her of her hated enemy!
 Let her not clothe in a religious garb

The bloody daring of licentious might!
Let her dare to seem the thing she is!
Exit.

SCENE 8

BURLEIGH, PAULET

BURLEIGH. She scorns us, she defies us, will defy us
Even at the scaffold's foot.

PAULET.   And yet, my lord,
Irregularities have been allowed
In these proceedings: Babington and Ballard
Should have been brought, with Curl and Nau, her servants,
Before her, face to face.

BURLEIGH.   No, Paulet, no,
That was not to be risked. Her influence
Upon the human heart is too supreme.
Her secretary Curl would straight shrink back
And fearfully revoke his own confession.

PAULET. Then England's enemies will fill the world
With rumours. These proceedings to the minds
Of all will signalize an act of outrage.

BURLEIGH. Had but this lovely mischief died before
She set her faithless foot on English ground!

PAULET. Amen, say I!

BURLEIGH.   Had sickness but consumed her—

PAULET. England had been secured from such misfortune!

BURLEIGH. And yet, if she had died in nature's course,
The world would still have called us murderers.

PAULET. 'Tis true, the world will think, despite of us,
Whatever it likes.

BURLEIGH.   Yet could it not be proved,
And it would make less noise.

PAULET.   Why, let it make
What noise it may! It is not clamorous blame,
But only righteous censure that can wound.

BURLEIGH. We know that holy justice cannot escape
The voice of censure, and the public cry
Is ever on the side of the unhappy.
The sword of justice, which adorns the man,
Is hateful in a woman's hand; the world
Will give no credit to a woman's justice,
If woman be the victim. Vain that we,
The judges, spoke what conscience dictated:
She has the royal privilege of mercy.

PAULET. And therefore——?

BURLEIGH.   Should she live? No! She should not!
'Tis this disturbs the Queen, whose eyes demand:
"Who'll save me from this sad alternative:
Either to tremble in eternal fear
Upon my throne or else to sacrifice
A queen of my own kindred on the block?"

PAULET. 'Tis even so, nor can it be avoided——

BURLEIGH. Well might it be avoided, thinks the Queen,
If she had only more attentive servants.

PAULET. How more attentive?

BURLEIGH.   Such as could interpret
A silent mandate.

PAULET.   What? A silent mandate?

BURLEIGH. Who, when a poisonous adder is delivered
Into their hands, would keep the treacherous charge
As if it were a sacred, precious jewel?

PAULET. A precious jewel is the Queen's good name;
One cannot guard it with sufficient care.

BURLEIGH. When, out of Shrewsbury's hand, the Queen of
      Scots
Was trusted to Sir Amias Paulet's care——

PAULET. Let me not think I am indebted for it
To anything but my unblemished name!

BURLEIGH. Spread the report she wastes; grows sicker still
And sicker; and expires at last in peace.

Thus will she perish in the world's remembrance;
And your good name is pure.

PAULET.   But not my conscience.

A pause.

BURLEIGH. Though you refuse us, sir, your own assistance,
You will not, sure, prevent another's hand?

PAULET. Her life's a sacred trust. To me the head
Of Queen Elizabeth is not more sacred.
Ye are the judges; judge, and break the staff;
And when 'tis time, then let the carpenter
With axe and saw appear to build the scaffold;
My castle's portals shall be open to him,
The sheriff, and the executioners.
Till then, she is entrusted to my care.

Exeunt.

ACT II

SCENE 1

LONDON. A HALL IN THE PALACE OF WESTMINSTER

The EARL OF KENT *and* SIR WILLIAM DAVISON, *meeting.*

DAVISON. Is that my lord of Kent? So soon returned?
  Is then the tourney, the carousal over?

KENT. How now? Were you not present at the tilt?

DAVISON. My office kept me here.

KENT.   You have missed
  The fairest show which ever taste devised:
  For *Beauty's* virgin fortress was presented,
  As by *Desire* assaulted. The Earl Marshal,
  The Lord High Admiral, and ten other knights
  Belonging to the Queen, defended it,
  And France's cavaliers led the attack.
  A herald marched before the gallant troop
  And summoned, in a madrigal, the fortress;
  And from the walls the chancellor replied;
  And then the artillery played, and nosegays,
  Breathing delicious fragrance, were discharged
  From pretty cannons; but in vain, the storm
  Was valiantly resisted, and *Desire*
  Was forced, unwillingly, to raise the siege.

DAVISON. A sign of evil boding, good my lord,
  For the French suitors.

KENT.   Why, you know that this
  Was but in sport; when the attack's in earnest,
  The fortress will, no doubt, capitulate.

DAVISON. Ha! Think you so? I never can believe it.

KENT. The hardest article of all is now

Adjusted and acceded to by France:
The Duke of Anjou is content to hold
Catholic worship in a private chapel,
And publicly he promises to honour
And to protect the realm's established faith.
Had you but heard the people's joyful shouts
Wherever the tidings spread! For it has been
The country's constant fear the Queen might die
Without immediate issue of her body,
And England bear again the Romish chains
If Mary Stuart should ascend the throne.

DAVISON. This fear appears superfluous: she goes
Into the bridal chamber; Mary Stuart
Enters the gates of death.

KENT.   The Queen approaches.

SCENE 2

Enter ELIZABETH, *led in by* LEICESTER, COUNTS AUBESPINE,
BELLIÈVRE, LORDS SHREWSBURY *and* BURLEIGH, *with other
French and English Gentlemen.*

ELIZABETH, *to* AUBESPINE.
Count Aubespine, I know how you must miss
The sparkling splendour of St. Germain's court.
Such pompous festivals of godlike state
I cannot furnish as the royal court
Of France. A sober and contented people
Which crowd around me with a thousand blessings
Whenever I present myself in public:
This is the spectacle which I can show,
And not without some pride, to foreign eyes.
The splendour of the noble dames who bloom
In Catherine's beauteous garden would, I know,
Eclipse myself and my more modest merits.

AUBESPINE. The court of England has one lady only
To show the wondering foreigner, but all
That charms our hearts in the accomplished sex
Is seen united in her single person.

BELLIÈVRE. Great Majesty of England, suffer us
　　To take our leave, and to our royal master,
　　The Duke of Anjou, bring the happy news.

ELIZABETH. Press me no further now, Count Bellièvre,
　　It is not now a time, I must repeat,
　　To kindle here the joyful marriage torch.
　　A fatal blow is aimed against my heart.

BELLIÈVRE. We only ask Your Majesty to promise
　　Your royal hand when brighter days shall come.

ELIZABETH. My wish was ever to remain unmarried
　　That men hereafter on my tomb might read:
　　"Here rests the Virgin Queen." But my subjects think
　　And clamorously assert, 'tis not enough
　　That blessings now are showered upon this land,
　　They ask a sacrifice for future welfare:
　　That I should cede my virgin liberty,
　　To satisfy my people. 'Tis by this
　　I see that I am nothing but a woman
　　In their regard; and yet methought that I
　　Had governed like a man, yes, like a king.
　　Well know I that it is not serving God
　　To quit the laws of nature; and that those
　　Who here have ruled before me merit praise
　　For opening the cloister gates and giving
　　Thousands of victims of ill-taught devotion
　　Back to the duties of humanity . . .
　　But yet a Queen, who has not spent her days
　　In fruitless, idle contemplation; who,
　　Without a murmur, indefatigably,
　　Performs the hardest of all duties; *she*
　　Should be exempted from that natural law
　　Which does ordain one half of humankind
　　Shall ever be subservient to the other.

AUBESPINE. Great Queen, you have upon your throne done
　　　　honour
　　To every virtue; nothing now remains
　　But to the sex whose greatest boast you are
　　To be the leading star and great example.
　　'Tis true, the man exists not who deserves you,

Yet if there were a prince alive to-day
Deserving of this honour——

ELIZABETH.   Without doubt,
My Lord Ambassador, a marriage union
With France's royal son would do me honour.
If I must yield unto my people's prayers,
I do not know in Europe any prince
To whom with less reluctance I would yield.
Let this confession satisfy your master.

BELLIÈVRE. It gives the fairest hope, and yet it gives
Nothing but hope; my master wishes more.

ELIZABETH *takes a ring from her finger and examines it.*
This common token marks one common duty,
One common servitude; the ring denotes
Marriage; and 'tis of rings a chain is formed.
Convey this present to His Highness. 'Tis
As yet no chain; it binds me not as yet;
But out of it may grow a link to bind me.

BELLIÈVRE, *kneeling.* This present I receive and press the kiss
Of homage on the hand of her who is
Henceforth my princess.

ELIZABETH, *to the* EARL OF LEICESTER, *whom she, during the
last speeches, had continually regarded.*

                         By your leave, my lord.

She takes the Order of the Garter from his neck and invests
BELLIÈVRE *with it.*

Invest His Highness with this ornament.
"*Honi soit qui mal y pense.*" So be it.
And let the bond of confidence unite
Henceforth the crowns of Britain and of France.

BELLIÈVRE. See! mercy beams upon your radiant brow:
Let the reflection of its cheering light
Fall on a wretched princess who concerns
Britain and France alike!

ELIZABETH.   No further, Count.
Let us not mix two inconsistent things:
If France be truly anxious for my hand,

It must partake my interests and renounce
Alliance with my foes.

AUBESPINE.   In your own eyes
Would she not seem to act unworthily
If in this joyous treaty she forgot
That hapless Queen, the widow of her King?

ELIZABETH. France has discharged her duties as a friend.
I will fulfil my own as England's Queen.

She bows to the French AMBASSADORS, *who, with the other Gentlemen, retire respectfully.*

SCENE 3

Enter BURLEIGH, LEICESTER, *and* SHREWSBURY. *The* QUEEN *takes her seat.*

BURLEIGH. Illustrious sovereign, you crown to-day
The fervent wishes of a loyal people.
Now but one only care disturbs this land:
It is a sacrifice which every voice
Demands. Oh, grant but this, and England's peace
Will be established now and evermore.

ELIZABETH. What wish is this, my lord? Speak.

BURLEIGH.   They demand
The Stuart's head. If to your people you
Wouldst now secure the precious boon of freedom
And the fair light of truth so dearly won
Then she must die. If we are not to live
In endless terror for your precious life
The enemy must fall. For well you know
Romish idolatry still has its friends
In secret in this island, and they're leagued
With the fell Cardinal of Guise, her uncle.
Rheims is his see and Rheims his arsenal.
Rheims is the Guise's school of regicide.
Thence come their missionary spies. From thence
Have we not seen the third assassin come?
While in her castle sits, at Fotheringay,

The Ate of this everlasting war
And with a torch of love sets fire to all.
To set her free, young men resolve to die.
To set her free? That's a pretence. The aim
Is to establish her upon your throne!

ELIZABETH. Lord Burleigh, there is wisdom in your speech
And yet I hate this wisdom when it calls
For blood. I hate it in my inmost soul.
Think of a milder counsel. Good my Lord
Of Shrewsbury, we crave your judgement here.

SHREWSBURY. Long may you live, my Queen, to be our joy!
Never hath this isle beheld such happy days
Since it was governed by its native kings.
Ere it shall buy its happiness with its
Good name, may Talbot's eyes be closed in death!

ELIZABETH. Forbid it, Heaven, that our good name be stained!

SHREWSBURY. Then must you find some other way than this
To save your kingdom, for the sentence passed
Of death against the Stuart is unjust.
You cannot upon her pronounce a sentence
Who is not subject to you.

ELIZABETH.   Then, it seems,
My council and my parliament have erred:
Each bench of justice in the land is wrong,
Which did with one accord admit this right.

SHREWSBURY, *after a pause.*
The proof of justice lies not in the voice
Of numbers. England's not the world nor is
Your parliament a focus to collect
The vast opinion of the human race.
This present England is no more the future,
Than 'tis the past; as inclination changes,
Thus ever ebbs and flows the unstable tide
Of public judgement. Do not say that you
Must act as stern necessity compels,
That you must yield to the importunate
Petitions of your people. Every hour
You can experience that your will is free.
Make trial and declare that you hate blood

And that you will protect your sister's life,
And you shall see how stern necessity
Can vanish, and what once was titled justice
Into injustice be converted.

A pause.

Yourself must pass the sentence, you alone.
God has not planted rigour in the frame
Of woman; and the founders of this realm,
Who to the female hand have not denied
The reins of government, intend by this
To show that mercy, not severity,
Is the best virtue to adorn a crown.

ELIZABETH. Lord Shrewsbury is a fervent advocate
For mine and England's enemy. I must
Prefer those counsellors who wish *my* welfare.

SHREWSBURY. I do not take the part of her misdeeds.
They say 'twas she who planned her husband's murder;
'Tis true that she espoused his murderer.
A grievous crime this was but then it happened
In the stern agony of civil war.
God knows what arts were used to overcome her!
For woman is a weak and fragile thing.

ELIZABETH. Woman's not weak! There are heroic souls
Among the sex, and in my presence, sir,
I do forbid to speak of woman's weakness.

SHREWSBURY. Misfortune was for you a rigid school,
You were not stationed on the sunny side
Of life, you saw no throne from far before you:
The grave was gaping for you at your feet.
The father of this land taught you your duty
At Woodstock and in London's gloomy Tower.
No flatterer sought you there: far from the world
Your soul learnt there to commune with itself
And estimate the real goods of life.
How different was the lot of that poor woman:
Transplanted in her youth to giddy France
She was deluded by the glare of vice
And carried forward on the stream of ruin.
Hers was the vain possession of a face;

For she outshone all others of her sex
As much in beauty as nobility.

ELIZABETH. Those charms must surely be without compare
Which can engender, in an elder's blood,
Such fire!

A pause.

My lord of Leicester, you are silent.

LEICESTER. Astonishment possesses me, I own,
To think this queen who, in her days of freedom,
Was but your puppet should, as your prisoner,
Be so formidable. What makes her so?
That she lays claim to England? That the Guises
Will not acknowledge you as England's queen?
And is not she, by Henry's will, passed over
In silence? Is it probable that England
Should throw itself into this papist's arms?
From you, the sovereign it adores, desert
To Darnley's murderess? What will they then,
These restless men who even in your lifetime
Torment you with a successor, who cannot
Dispose of you in marriage soon enough
To rescue church and state from fancied peril?
Stand you not blooming there in youthful prime
While each step leads her towards the expecting tomb?
By heaven, I hope you will full many a year
Walk over the Stuart's grave and never be
Yourself the instrument of her sad end.

BURLEIGH. Lord Leicester hath not always held this tone.

LEICESTER. 'Tis true I in the court of justice gave
My verdict for her death; here in the council
I may consistently speak otherwise.
Here, right is not the question but advantage.
Is this a time to fear her power when France,
Her succour, has abandoned her, and you
Prepare to give your hand to France's son?
Then hasten not her death: she's dead already.
Contempt and scorn are death to her; take heed
Lest ill-timed pity call her into life.
'Tis therefore my advice to leave the sentence

By which her life is forfeit in full force.
Let her live on, but let her live beneath
The headsman's axe, and, at the very hour
Aught is attempted for her, let it fall.

ELIZABETH *rises.*

My lords, I now have heard your several thoughts.
With God's help, I will weigh your arguments
And choose what best my judgement shall approve.

SCENE 4

Enter SIR AMIAS PAULET *and* MORTIMER.

ELIZABETH. Sir Amias Paulet! Well, noble sir,
What tidings bring you?

PAULET.   Gracious Sovereign,
My nephew, who but lately is returned
From foreign travel, kneels before your feet
And offers you his first and earliest homage.

MORTIMER, *kneeling on one knee.*
Long live my royal mistress! Happiness
And glory form a crown to grace her brows!

ELIZABETH. Arise, Sir Knight; and welcome here in England.
You've made the tour I hear, have been in France
And Rome, and tarried too some time at Rheims.
Tell me what plots our enemies are hatching.

MORTIMER. May God confound them all, my gracious liege.

ELIZABETH. Did you see Morgan and the wily Bishop
Of Ross?

MORTIMER. I saw, my Queen, all Scottish exiles
Who forge at Rheims their plots against this realm.

PAULET. Private despatches they entrusted to him,
In ciphers, for the Queen of Scots, which he
With loyal hand hath given up to us.

ELIZABETH. Say, what are then their latest plans of treason?

MORTIMER. It struck them all as 'twere a thunderbolt
That France should leave them and with England close

This firm alliance. Now they turn their hopes
Towards Spain——

ELIZABETH.   This Walsingham has written us.

LEICESTER. England no more is frightened by such arms.

BURLEIGH. They're always dangerous in bigots' hands.

ELIZABETH, *looking steadfastly at* MORTIMER.
Your enemies have said that you frequented
The schools at Rheims and have abjured your faith.

MORTIMER. So I pretended, that I must confess:
Such was my anxious wish to serve my Queen.

ELIZABETH, *to* PAULET, *who presents papers to her.*
What have you there?

PAULET.   'Tis from the Queen of Scots.
'Tis a petition, and addressed to you.

BURLEIGH, *hastily catching at it.* Give it to me.

PAULET, *giving it to the* QUEEN.   My lord, she ordered me
To bring it to Her Majesty's own hands.
    The QUEEN *takes the letter: as she reads it,* MORTIMER *and*
    LEICESTER *speak some words in private.*

BURLEIGH, *to* PAULET.
Idle complaints, from which one ought to screen
The Queen's too tender heart.

PAULET.   She asks a boon.
She begs to be admitted to the grace
Of speaking with the Queen.

BURLEIGH.   It cannot be.

SHREWSBURY. Why not? Her supplication's not unjust.

BURLEIGH. For her, the base encourager of murder,
Her who has thirsted for our sovereign's blood——

SHREWSBURY. And if the Queen is gracious, sir, are you
The man to hinder pity's soft emotion?

BURLEIGH. She is condemned to death; 'twould ill become
The Queen to see a death-devoted head.
The sentence cannot have its execution
If the Queen's majesty approaches her
For pardon still attends the royal presence.

ELIZABETH, *having read the letter, dries her tears.*

Oh, what is man? What is the bliss of earth?
To what extremities is she reduced
Who with such proud and splendid hopes began?
Who, called to sit on the most ancient throne
Of Christendom, misled by vain ambition,
Hoped with a triple crown to deck her brows?
How is her language altered since the time
When she assumed the arms of England's crown
And by the flatterers of her Court was styled
Sole monarch of the two Britannic isles!
Forgive me, lords, my heart is cleft in twain
To think that earthly goods are so unstable
And that the dreadful fate which rules mankind
Should threaten mine own house and scowl so near me!

SHREWSBURY. Stretch forth your hand, to raise this abject
        Queen,
    And, like the luminous figure of an angel,
    Descend into her gaol's sepulchral night!

BURLEIGH. Be steadfast, mighty Queen. Let no emotion
    Of seeming laudable humanity
    Mislead you. Take not from yourself the power
    Of acting as necessity commands.

LEICESTER. The law of England, not the monarch's will,
    Condemns the Queen of Scotland, and 'twere worthy
    Of the great soul of Queen Elizabeth
    To follow the soft dictates of her heart.
    But the Queen's wise and does not need our counsel.

ELIZABETH. Retire, my lords. We shall, perhaps, find means
    To reconcile the tender claims of pity
    With what necessity imposes on us.
    But now retire——

    The LORDS *retire. She calls* SIR EDWARD MORTIMER *back.*
            Sir Edward Mortimer!

SCENE 5

ELIZABETH, MORTIMER

ELIZABETH, *having measured him for some time, with her eyes, in silence.*
He who has timely learnt to play so well
The difficult dissembler's needful task
Becomes a perfect man before his time.
Fate calls you to a lofty scene of action:
I prophesy it and can, happily
For you, fulfil myself my own prediction.

MORTIMER. Illustrious mistress, what I am and all
I can accomplish is devoted to you.

ELIZABETH. You've made acquaintance with the foes of
England.
Their hate against me is implacable;
Their fell designs are inexhaustible.
As yet, indeed, almighty Providence
Has shielded me, but on my brows the crown
Forevér trembles while *she* lives who fans
Their bigot zeal and animates their hopes.

MORTIMER. She lives no more as soon as you command it.

ELIZABETH. The sentence is pronounced—what gain I by it?
It must be executed, Mortimer,
And I must authorize the execution.
The blame will ever light on me. I must
Avow it nor can save appearances.
That is the worst——

MORTIMER.   But can appearances
Disturb your conscience where the cause is just?

ELIZABETH. You are unpractised in the world, Sir Knight.
What we appear is subject to the judgement
Of all mankind, but what we are, of no man.
No one will be convinced that I am right:

I must take care that my connivance in
Her death be wrapped in everlasting doubt.

MORTIMER, *seeking to learn her meaning.*
Then it perhaps were best——

ELIZABETH, *quickly.*   Ay, surely 'twere
The best; my better angel speaks through you.
You are in earnest; you examine deep;
Have quite a different spirit from your uncle.

MORTIMER, *surprised.*
Have you imparted then your wishes to him?

ELIZABETH. I am sorry that I have.

MORTIMER.   Excuse his age.
The old man is grown scrupulous, I fear.
My hand I'll lend you; save then as you can
Your reputation——

ELIZABETH.   Well, sir, if you could
But waken me some morning with the news:
"This Mary Stuart, your bloodthirsty foe,
Breathed yesternight her last"——

MORTIMER.   Depend on me.

ELIZABETH. When shall my head lie calmly down to sleep?

MORTIMER. The next new moon will terminate your fears.

ELIZABETH. And be the selfsame happy day the dawn
Of your preferment. So God speed you, sir.
Be not aggrieved, sir, that my gratitude
Must wear the mask of darkness. Silence is
The happy suitor's god. The closest bonds,
The dearest, are the work of secrecy.
Exit.

SCENE 6

MORTIMER, *alone*

MORTIMER. Go, false deceitful Queen! As you delude
The world, even so I cozen you; 'tis right,
Thus to betray you; 'tis a worthy deed.

Trust only to my arm and keep your own
Concealed; assume the pious outward show
Of mercy 'fore the world, while reckoning
In secret on my murderous aid; and thus
By gaining time we shall ensure *her* rescue.
You will exalt me, show me from afar
The costly recompense, but even were
Yourself the prize and all your woman's favour,
What are you, poor one, and what can you proffer?
I scorn ambition's avaricious strife.
With her, with her, is all the charm of life!
I can effect her rescue, I alone.
Be danger, honour, and the prize my own!
—I must attend Lord Leicester and deliver
Her letter to him—'tis a hateful charge—
I have no confidence in this court puppet—

As he is going, PAULET *meets him.*

SCENE 7

MORTIMER, PAULET

PAULET. What said the Queen to you?
MORTIMER.   'Twas nothing, sir,
   Nothing of consequence—
PAULET, *looking at him earnestly.*
                              Hear, Mortimer!
   It is slippery ground on which you tread.
   I know the deed the Queen proposed to you.
   Have you then pledged your promise, have you?—
MORTIMER.   Uncle!
PAULET. If you have done so, I abandon you,
   And lay my curse upon you—
LEICESTER, *entering.*   Worthy sir!
   I with your nephew wish a word. The Queen
   Is graciously inclined to him. She wills
   That to his custody the Scottish queen

Be with full powers entrusted. She relies
On his fidelity.

PAULET.   The Queen relies
On him; and I, my noble lord, rely
Upon myself and my two open eyes.
Exit.

SCENE 8

LEICESTER, MORTIMER

LEICESTER, *surprised.* What ailed the knight?

MORTIMER.   The confidence, perhaps,
The Queen so suddenly confers on me.

LEICESTER. Are you deserving, then, of confidence?

MORTIMER. That would I ask of you, my lord of Leicester.

LEICESTER. You said you wished to speak with me in private.

MORTIMER. Assure me first that I may safely venture.

LEICESTER. I see you, sir, exhibit at this court
Two different aspects. One of them must be
A borrowed one, but which of them is real?

MORTIMER. The selfsame doubts I have concerning you.

LEICESTER. Who then shall pave the way to confidence?

MORTIMER. He who, by doing it, is least in danger.

LEICESTER. Well, that are you——

MORTIMER.   No, you! The evidence
Of such a weighty, powerful peer as you
Can overwhelm my voice. My accusations
Were weak against your rank and influence.

LEICESTER. Sir, you mistake. In everything but this
I'm powerful here, but in this tender point
Which I am called upon to trust you with
The poorest testimony can undo me.

MORTIMER. If the all-powerful Earl of Leicester deign
To stoop so low to meet me, and to make

Such a confession to me, I may venture
To think a little better of myself.

Producing suddenly the letter.

Here is a letter from the Queen of Scotland.

LEICESTER, *alarmed, catches hastily at the letter.*
Speak softly, sir! What see I?—— Oh, it is
Her picture!——

Kisses and examines it with speechless joy. A pause.

MORTIMER, *who has watched him closely the whole time.*
Now, my lord, I can believe you.

LEICESTER, *having run hastily through the letter.*
You know the purport of this letter, sir?

MORTIMER. Not I.

LEICESTER. She surely has informed you——

MORTIMER. She said
You would explain this riddle to me—— 'Tis
To me a riddle that the Earl of Leicester,
The far-famed favourite of Elizabeth,
The open, bitter enemy of Mary,
Should be the man from whom the Queen expects
Deliverance from her woes; and yet it must be.
Your eyes express too plainly what your heart
Feels for the hapless lady.

LEICESTER. Tell me, sir,
First, how it comes that you should take so warm
An interest in her fate; and what it was
Gained you her confidence?

MORTIMER. My lord, I can:
A letter from the Cardinal Archbishop
Was my credential with the Queen of Scots.

LEICESTER. Each remnant of distrust be henceforth banished!
Your hand, sir; pardon me these idle doubts.
Knowing how Walsingham and Burleigh hate me
And, watching me, in secret spread their snares,
I feared you were their instrument, their creature,
To lure me to their toils.

MORTIMER. How poor a part

　　So great a nobleman is forced to play
　　At court! My lord, I pity you.

LEICESTER.　　　　　　　　With joy
　　I rest upon the faithful breast of friendship.
　　You seem surprised, sir, that my heart is turned
　　So suddenly towards the captive Queen.
　　In truth, I never hated her; the times
　　Have forced me to appear her enemy.
　　She was, as you well know, my destined bride
　　Long since, ere she bestowed her hand on Darnley,
　　While yet the beams of glory round her smiled.
　　Coldly I then refused the proffered boon.
　　Now, at the hazard of my life, I claim her,
　　Though she's confined and at the brink of death.

MORTIMER. True magnanimity, my lord of Leicester.

LEICESTER. Ambition made me all insensible
　　To youth and beauty. Mary's hand I held
　　Too insignificant for me. I hoped
　　To be the husband of the Queen of England.

MORTIMER. It is well known she gave you preference
　　Before all others.

LEICESTER.　　　　So, indeed, it seems.
　　Men call me happy!—— Did they only know
　　What the chains are for which they envy me!
　　For I have sacrificed ten bitter years
　　To the proud idol of her vanity,
　　Submitted with a slave's humility
　　To every change of her despotic fancies,
　　The plaything of each little wayward whim.
　　At times by seeming tenderness caressed,
　　As oft repulsed with proud and cold disdain,
　　Alike tormented by her grace and rigour,
　　Watched like a prisoner by the Argus eyes
　　Of jealousy, examined like a schoolboy,
　　And railed at like a servant—— Oh, no tongue
　　Can paint this hell!

MORTIMER.　　　　　My lord, I feel for you.

LEICESTER. To lose, and at the very goal, the prize!
　　'Tis not her hand alone this envious stranger

Threatens, he'd rob me of her favour too:
She is a woman, and he, formed to please.

MORTIMER. He is the son of Catherine. He has learnt,
In a good school, the arts of flattery.

LEICESTER. As fall these hopes, I turn towards the hope
Of former days. Within me Mary's image
Renews itself, and youth reclaims its rights.
No more 'tis cold ambition; from my heart
I yearn to have my jewel back again.
I have already sent the Queen the news
Of my conversion to her interests,
And in this letter which you brought me she
Assures me that she pardons me and offers,
If I rescue her, herself as guerdon.

MORTIMER. But you attempted nothing for her rescue.
You let her be condemned without a word.
You voted for her death——

LEICESTER.　　　　　　　　　I was obliged,
Before the world, to persecute her still,
But do not think that I would patiently
Have seen her led to death. No, sir, I hoped,
And still I hope, to ward off all extremes,
Till I can find some certain means to save her.

MORTIMER. These are already found: my lord of Leicester,
Your generous confidence in me deserves
A like return. *I* will deliver her.

LEICESTER. What say you? You alarm me—— How?—— You
would——?

MORTIMER. I'll open forcibly her prison gates.
I have confederates, and all is ready.

LEICESTER. Alas, in what rash enterprise would you
Engage me? And these friends, know they *my* secret?

MORTIMER. Fear not. Our plan was laid without your help.
Without your help it would have been accomplished
Had she not signified her resolution
To owe her liberty to you alone.

LEICESTER. And can you then with certainty assure me
That in your plot my name has not been mentioned?

MORTIMER. You wish to rescue Mary and possess her;
You find confederates; sudden, unexpected,
The readiest means fall, as it were, from heaven;
Yet you show more perplexity than joy.

LEICESTER. We must avoid all violence. It is
Too dangerous an enterprise.

MORTIMER.   Delay
Is also dangerous.

LEICESTER.   I tell you, sir,
It is not to be attempted——

MORTIMER.   It is
Too hazardous for you who would possess her,
But we, who only wish to rescue her,
We are more bold.

LEICESTER.   You will not weigh the matter.
With blind and hasty rashness you destroy
The plans which I so happily had framed.

MORTIMER. And what were, then, the plans which you had
    framed?
And how, if I were miscreant enough
To murder her as was proposed to me
This moment by Elizabeth, and which
She looks upon as certain, only name
The measures you have taken to protect her?

LEICESTER. Did the Queen give you then this bloody order?

MORTIMER. She was deceived in me, as Mary is
In you.

LEICESTER. And have you promised it? Say, have you?

MORTIMER. That she might not engage another's hand,
I offered mine.

LEICESTER.   Well done, sir, that was right.
This gives us leisure, for she rests secure
Upon your bloody service; and the sentence
Is unfulfilled the while and we gain time.

MORTIMER, *angrily.* No, we are losing time!

LEICESTER.   The Queen depends
On you and will the readier make a show
Of mercy—so may I prevail on her

To give an audience to her adversary.
And by this stratagem we tie her hands.

MORTIMER. And what is gained by that? When she discovers
That I am cheating her, that Mary lives,
Are we not where we were? She never will
Be free. The mildest doom which can await her
At best is but perpetual confinement.
A daring deed must one day end the matter:
Why will you not with such a deed begin?
Fight a good fight for her! You know you are
Lord of the person of the Queen of England.
Invite her to your castle. She's been there
Before. Then show that you're a man. Keep her
Confined till she release our Queen!

LEICESTER.   Know you
The deeps and shallows of this court? Know you
The potent spell this female sceptre casts
Upon men's minds? In vain you seek the old
Heroic energy of this our land:
A woman holds it under lock and key——
Someone approaches. Go!

MORTIMER.   Yet Mary hopes!
Shall I return to her with empty comfort?

LEICESTER. Bear her my vows of everlasting love!

MORTIMER. Bear them yourself! I offered my assistance
As her deliverer not your messenger.
Exit.

SCENE 9

ELIZABETH, LEICESTER

ELIZABETH. Was someone here? I heard the sound of voices.

LEICESTER, *turning quickly and perplexedly round, on hearing
the* QUEEN. It was young Mortimer——

ELIZABETH.   How now, my lord!
Why so confused?

LEICESTER, *collecting himself.*
                    Your presence is the cause.
My sight is dazzled by your heavenly charms.
Oh!——

ELIZABETH. Whence this sigh?

LEICESTER.   Have I no reason, then,
    To sigh? When I behold you in your glory,
    I feel anew, with pain unspeakable,
    The loss which threatens me.

ELIZABETH.   What loss, my lord?

LEICESTER. Anjou has never seen you, can but love
    Your splendour and the splendour of your reign;
    But I love you, and were you born of all
    The peasant maids the poorest, I, the first
    Of kings, would lay my sceptre at your feet.

ELIZABETH. Pity me, Dudley; 'tis not my fortune
    To place upon the brows of him, the dearest
    Of men to me, the royal crown of England.
    The Queen of Scotland was allowed to make
    Her hand the token of her inclination;
    She has had every freedom, and has drunk,
    Even to the very dregs, the cup of joy.

LEICESTER. And now she drinks the bitter cup of sorrow.

ELIZABETH. She never did respect the world's opinion.
    Life was to her a sport; she never courted
    The yoke to which I bowed my willing neck.
    And yet, methinks, I had as just a claim
    As she to please myself and taste the joys
    Of life. But I preferred the rigid duties
    Which royalty imposed on me. Yet she,
    She was the favourite of all the men,
    And youth and age became alike her suitors.
    Thus are the men—voluptuaries all!
    For did not even Talbot, though grey-headed,
    Grow young again when speaking of her charms?

LEICESTER. Forgive him. Talbot was her keeper once,
    And she has fooled him with her cunning wiles.

ELIZABETH. And is it really true that she's so fair?

Pictures are flattering, and description lies:
I will trust nothing but my own conviction.
Why gaze you at me thus?

LEICESTER.   I placed in thought
You and this Mary Stuart side by side.
Yes! I confess, I oft have felt a wish,
If it could be but secretly contrived,
To see you placed beside the Scottish Queen.
Then would you feel, and not till then, the full
Enjoyment of your triumph. She deserves
To be thus humbled. She deserves to see
Herself surpassed, to feel herself overmatched.

ELIZABETH. In years she has the advantage——

LEICESTER.   Has she so?
I never should have thought it. Can her griefs
Have brought down age upon her ere her time?
And it would mortify her more to see you
As bride. She has already turned her back
On each fair hope of life and she would see you
Advancing towards the open arms of joy!

ELIZABETH, *with a careless air.*
I'm teased to grant this interview.

LEICESTER.   She asks it
As a favour; grant it as a punishment.
For though you should conduct her to the block,
Yet would it less torment her than to see
Herself extinguished by your beauty's splendour.
Thus can you murder her, as she has wished
To murder you. Could she but see your beauty,
Exalted by the splendour of the crown
And blooming so with tender bridal graces,
Now were the hour of her destruction come!

ELIZABETH. Now? No—not now. No, Leicester, this must be
Maturely weighed. I must with Burleigh——

LEICESTER.   Burleigh!
To him you are but sovereign, and as such
Alone he seeks your welfare. But your rights,
Derived from womanhood, this tender point
Must be decided by your own tribunal!

ELIZABETH. But would it then become me to behold
My kinswoman in infamy and want?

LEICESTER. You need not cross her threshold. Hear my counsel.
The hunt you mean to honour with your presence
Is in the neighbourhood of Fotheringay.
Permission may be given to Lady Stuart
To take the air. You meet her in the park,
As if by accident.

ELIZABETH, *after a pause.*

           I should not care
To cross your merest whim, for I have grieved you.
And may not our affection grant more than
We do approve? But let it be—your whim.

She speaks the last sentence with tenderness. LEICESTER
prostrates himself before her.

ACT III

SCENE 1

OUTSIDE THE CASTLE OF FOTHERINGAY

In the foreground, trees; in the background, a distant prospect

MARY *advances, running from behind the trees.* HANNAH
KENNEDY *follows slowly.*

KENNEDY. You fly before, my lady, as on wings.

MARY. *Let me enjoy my new-found liberty!*
Let us be children! Be a child with me!
We'll find the wingèd step of youth again
Upon the verdant carpet of the plain!
　　　I have escaped the prison's sadness
　　　　　And left behind the house of care!
　　　O, let me in my hungry gladness
　　　　　Drink in the free, celestial air!

KENNEDY. Your gaol has been extended but a little.
The walls are barely hidden by those trees.

MARY. *I thank you, friendly trees, that hide from me*
　　　My darksome prison's dread seclusion!
I fain would dream myself happy and free!
　　　Why wake me from my dream's illusion?
Free and unfettered are my eyes!
The vault of heaven about me lies.
Space is a wide immeasurable sea.
　　　There, where the misty mountains soar,
I can my Scotland's boundary descry,
While the swift clouds that southward fly
　　　Seek the French kingdom's distant shore!

KENNEDY. Fond, fruitless wishes! See you not from far
How we are followed by observing spies?

MARY, *oblivious.* I recognise in this the mighty arm
  Of Leicester. They will by degrees expand
  My prison; will accustom me, through small,
  To greater liberty; until at last
  I'll see the face of him whose hand will dash
  My fetters off!

KENNEDY.   Their chains are also loosed
  Whom everlasting liberty awaits.

  Hunting horns are heard.

MARY. *O painful memory yet dear!*
  It ever was my joy to hear
  The hound and horn
  Salute the morn
  In the glens of the highlands, loud and clear!

SCENE 2

Enter PAULET.

PAULET. Well? Have I acted right at last, my lady?
  Do I for once, at least, deserve your thanks?

MARY. How? Do I owe this favour, sir, to you?

PAULET. Why not to me? I gave the Queen your letter.

MARY. And is this freedom which I now enjoy
  The happy consequence?

PAULET, *significantly.*
                    Nor that alone.
  You heard the hunting horns?

MARY, *starting back with apprehension.*
                    You frighten me!

PAULET. The Queen is hunting in the neighbourhood——

MARY, *gives a short cry.*

  In a few moments she'll appear before you.

KENNEDY, *hastening towards* MARY, *who is trembling and
  about to fall.* How fare you, dearest lady? You grow pale.

PAULET. Is it not well? Was it not then your prayer?

MARY. Now I am not prepared for it. Not now!
   What, as the greatest favour, I besought
   Seems to me now most fearful. Hannah, come,
   Lead me into the house till I collect
   My spirits.

PAULET.   Stay, you must await her here.

SCENE 3

Enter the EARL OF SHREWSBURY.

MARY. Worthy Shrewsbury! Save me from this sight!

SHREWSBURY. Command yourself, your Majesty. Have
      courage!
   'Tis the decisive moment of your fate.

MARY. For this I've studied, weighed, and written down
   Each word within the tablet of my memory
   That was to touch and move her to compassion.
   Yet nothing lives within me at this moment
   But the fierce, burning feeling of my wrongs!

SHREWSBURY. However much the inward struggle cost
   You must submit to stern necessity.
   The power is in *her* hand; therefore be humble.

MARY. To her? I never can.

SHREWSBURY.   Speak with respect
   And strive to move her magnanimity.
   Insist not now upon your rights, not now——

MARY. Rather in love could fire and water meet,
   The timid lamb embrace the roaring tiger!
   I have been hurt too grievously; she has
   Too grievously oppressed me. No atonement
   Can make us friends.

SHREWSBURY.   First see her, face to face.
   Did I not see how she was moved at reading
   Your letter? How her eyes were drowned in tears?

MARY, *seizing his hand.*
   They have indeed misused me, Shrewsbury.

SHREWSBURY. Let all be now forgot, and only think
How to receive her with submissiveness.

MARY. Is Burleigh with her too, my evil genius?

SHREWSBURY. No one attends her but the Earl of Leicester.

MARY. Lord Leicester?

SHREWSBURY.   Fear not him. It was his work
That here the Queen has granted you this meeting.

MARY. Ah, well I knew it!

SHREWSBURY.   What?

PAULET.   The Queen approaches.

They all draw aside; MARY *alone remains, leaning on*
KENNEDY.

SCENE 4

THE SAME

ELIZABETH, EARL OF LEICESTER, *and Retinue*

ELIZABETH, *to* LEICESTER. What seat is that, my lord?

LEICESTER.   'Tis Fotheringay.

ELIZABETH, *to* SHREWSBURY.
My lord, send back our retinue to London.
The people crowd too eager in the roads.
We'll seek a refuge in this quiet park.

TALBOT *sends the train away. She looks steadfastly at* MARY
as she speaks further with LEICESTER.

My honest people love me overmuch.
Thus should a god be honoured, not a mortal.

MARY, *who the whole time has leaned, almost fainting, on*
KENNEDY, *rises now, and her eyes meet the steady, piercing
look of* ELIZABETH; *she shudders and throws herself again
upon* KENNEDY'S *bosom.*
Alas, from out those features speaks no heart.

ELIZABETH. What lady's that?

A general, embarrassed silence.

LEICESTER.   You are at Fotheringay,
    My liege!

ELIZABETH, *as if surprised, casting an angry look at* LEICESTER.
        Who has done this, my lord of Leicester?

LEICESTER. 'Tis past, my Queen; and now that Heaven has led
    Your footsteps hither, be magnanimous!

SHREWSBURY. But cast your eyes on this unhappy one
    Who stands dissolved in anguish!

    MARY *collects herself and begins to advance towards* ELIZA-
    BETH, *stops, shuddering, halfway; her action expresses the
    most violent internal struggle.*

ELIZABETH.   How, my lords?
    Which of you had announced to me a prisoner
    Bowed down by woe? I see a haughty one
    In no way humbled by calamity.

MARY. Farewell high thought and pride of noble mind!
    I will forget my dignity and all
    My sufferings. I will fall before her feet
    Who has reduced me to this wretchedness.
    She turns towards the QUEEN.

    The voice of Heaven decides for you, my sister.
    Your happy brows are now with triumph crowned.
    I bless the Power Divine which thus has raised you.
    She kneels.

    But in your turn be merciful, my sister.
    Stretch forth your hand, your royal hand, to raise
    Your sister from the depths of her distress.

ELIZABETH, *stepping back.*
    You are where it becomes you, Lady Stuart,
    And thankfully I prize my God's protection
    Who has not suffered me to kneel a suppliant
    Thus at your feet as you now kneel at mine.

MARY, *with increasing energy of feeling.*
    Think on all earthly things, vicissitudes,
    For there are gods who punish haughty pride!
    Before these strangers' eyes, dishonour not
    Yourself in me! Profane not nor disgrace

The royal blood of Tudor! In my veins
It flows as pure a stream as in your own.
Oh, for God's pity, stand not so estranged
And inaccessible, like sóme tall cliff
Which shipwrecked sailors try to reach in vain.
My all, my life, my fortune now depend
Upon the influence of my words and tears.
That I may touch your heart, O set mine free!
If you regard me with those freezing looks
My shuddering heart contracts and turns to ice.

ELIZABETH, *cold and severe.*

What would you say to me, my lady Stuart?
You wished to speak with me; and I, forgetting
The Queen and all the wrongs I have sustained,
Fulfil the pious duty of the sister
And grant the boon you wished for of my presence.
Yet I, in yielding to the generous feelings
Of magnanimity, expose myself
To rightful censure that I stoop so low.
For well you know you would have had me murdered.

MARY. Oh, how shall I begin? Oh, how shall I
So artfully arrange my cautious words
That they may touch yet not offend your heart?
I cannot speak without impeaching you,
And that most heavily. I wish not so.
You have not, as you ought, behaved to me.
I am a Queen, like you, yet you have held me
Confined in prison. As a suppliant
I came to you, yet you in me insulted
The pious use of hospitality;
Slighting in me the holy law of nations,
Immured me in a dungeon; tore from me
My friends and servants. To unseemly want
I was exposed and hurried to the bar
Of a disgraceful, insolent tribunal.
No more of this! In everlasting silence
Be buried all the cruelties I suffered!
See—— I will throw the blame of all on fate.
An evil spirit rose from the abyss
To kindle in our hearts the flames of hatred.

It grew with us, and bad, designing men—
Frantic enthusiasts with sword and dagger—
Armed the uncalled-for hand. This is the curse
Of kings, that they, divided, tear the world
In pieces and let loose hell's raging furies!

Approaching her confidently, and with a flattering tone.

Now stand we face to face; now, sister, speak;
Name but my crime, I'll fully satisfy you.
Alas, had you vouchsafed to hear me then,
When I, so earnest, sought to meet your eye,
It never would have come to this, my sister—
This so distressful, this so mournful meeting!

ELIZABETH. Accuse not fate. Your own deceitful heart
It was, the wild ambition of your house.
As yet no enmities had passed between us
When your imperious uncle, the proud priest,
Whose shameless hand grasps at all crowns, attacked me
With unprovoked hostility and taught
You, but too docile, to assume my arms
And meet me in the lists in mortal strife.
What means employed he not to storm my throne?
The curses of the priests, the people's sword,
The dreadful weapons of religious frenzy——
Even here in my own kingdom's peaceful haunts
He fanned the flames of civil insurrection.
But God is with me, and the haughty priest
Has not maintained the field. The blow was aimed
Full at my head. But yours it is that falls!

MARY. I'm in the hand of Heaven. You never will
Exert so cruelly the power it gives you.

ELIZABETH. Who shall prevent me? Ha? Did not your uncle
Set all the kings of Europe the example—
How to conclude a peace with those they hate?
Be mine the school of Saint Bartholomew:
The church can break the bonds of every duty,
It consecrates the regicide, the traitor.
I only practise what your priests have taught.
Say, then, what surety can be offered me,
Should I magnanimously loose your chains?

MARY. Had you declared me heir to your dominions,
  As is my right, then gratitude and love
  In me had fixed, for you, a faithful friend
  And kinswoman.

ELIZABETH.   Your friendship is abroad,
  Your house is popery, the monk your brother.
  Name *you* my successor! Oh, treacherous snare!
  That in my life you might seduce my people,
  And when I——

MARY.   Sister, rule your realm in peace:
  I give up every claim to these domains.
  Alas, the pinions of my soul are lamed;
  Greatness entices me no more; your point
  Is gained. I am but Mary's shadow now.
  You have destroyed me in my bloom. Now speak
  The word which to pronounce has brought you hither.
  Pronounce this word. Say: "Mary, you are free.
  You have already felt my power, learn now
  To honour too my generosity."

ELIZABETH. So: you confess at last that you are conquered?
  Are all your schemes run out? No more assassins
  Now on the road? Will no adventurer
  Attempt again, for you, the sad achievement?
  Yes, madam, it is over. You'll seduce
  No mortal more. The world has other cares.
  None is ambitious of the dangerous honour
  Of being your fourth husband!

MARY, *starting angrily*.   Sister, sister!
  Grant me forbearance, all ye powers of heaven!

ELIZABETH *regards her long, with a look of proud contempt*.
  Those then, my Lord of Leicester, are the charms
  Which no man with impunity can view,
  Near which no woman dare attempt to stand?
  In sooth, this honour has been cheaply gained.
  She who to all is common may with ease
  Become the common object of applause!

MARY. This is too much!

ELIZABETH, *laughing insultingly*. You show us now, indeed,
  Your real face! Till now, 'twas but the mask!

MARY, *burning with rage, yet dignified and noble.*
My sins were human and the faults of youth.
Superior force misled me. I have never
Denied or sought to hide it. I despised
All false appearance as became a queen.
The worst of me is known, and I can say
That I am better than the fame I bear.
Woe to you when in time to come the world
Shall strip the robe of honour from your deeds!
Virtue was not your portion from your mother:
Well know we what it was that brought the head
Of Anne Boleyn down on the fatal block!

SHREWSBURY, *stepping between both* QUEENS.
Is this the moderation, the submission,
My lady?——

MARY.   Moderation! I've supported
What human nature can support. Farewell,
Lamb-hearted resignation, passive patience,
Fly to your native heaven! Burst at length
In all your fury, long-suppressèd rancour!

SHREWSBURY. She is distracted. My liege, forgive her.

ELIZABETH, *speechless with anger, casts enraged looks at*
MARY.

LEICESTER, *in the most violent agitation. He seeks to lead*
ELIZABETH *away.* Away from this disastrous place!

MARY, *raising her voice.*   A bastard
Profanes the English throne! The generous Britons
Are cheated by a juggler! Her whole person
Is false and painted—heart as well as face!
Into ELIZABETH'S *face.*
If right prevailed, you'd be lying in the dust
Before me! For I am your rightful queen!

ELIZABETH *hastily quits the stage; the* LORDS *follow her in
consternation.*

SCENE 5

MARY, KENNEDY

KENNEDY. Now all hope is over.

MARY, *still quite beside herself*. Gone hence in wrath!
Falling on KENNEDY's *bosom.*
Now I am happy, Hannah! Now, at last,
After whole years of sorrow and abasement,
One moment of victorious revenge!
A weight falls off my heart, a weight of mountains!

KENNEDY. Unhappy lady! Frenzy overcomes you!

MARY. I have abased her before Leicester's eyes.
How I did hurl her from her haughty height!
He saw it; he was witness of my triumph.

SCENE 6

Enter MORTIMER.

KENNEDY. Oh, sir! What a disaster!

MORTIMER.   I heard all——
*Gives the nurse a sign to repair to her post, and draws
nearer; his whole appearance expresses the utmost violence
of passion.*
Yours is the palm. You trod her in the dust.
Now I adore you as a deity!

MARY, *with vivacity and expectation.*
You spoke with Leicester? Gave my letter to him?

MORTIMER, *beholding her with glowing looks.*
Thou art the fairest woman upon earth!

MARY. What says his lordship? Say, sir, may I hope?

MORTIMER. Who? He?—— He is a wretch, a very coward!

MARY. What say you?

MORTIMER. He deliver and possess you?
Why, let him dare it! He! He must with me
In mortal contest first deserve the prize!

MARY. Will he do nothing for me?

MORTIMER. Speak not of him.
I will release you, I alone.

MARY. Alas,
What power have you?

MORTIMER. Deceive yourself no more.
The moment that the Queen thus quitted you,
And that your interview had taken this turn,
All hope was lost, each way of mercy shut.
You must be free before the morning break!

MARY. What say you, sir? To-night?— Impossible!

MORTIMER. Hear what has been resolved. I led my friends
Into a private chapel, where a priest
Heard our confession and, for every sin
We had committed, gave us absolution.
He gave us absolution too, beforehand,
For every crime we might commit in future.

MARY. Oh, God!

MORTIMER. We scale the castle walls to-night.
The keys are in our power. The guards we kill,
Then from your chamber bear you forcibly.
None must remain that might disclose the deed:
We'll murder every living soul—

MARY. But Paulet?
He'd sooner spill his dearest drop of blood—

MORTIMER. He falls the very first beneath my steel!

MARY. What, sir! Your uncle? What? Your second father?

MORTIMER. Must perish by my hand. I murder him.

MARY. Sin upon sin!

MORTIMER. No! We have been absolved
Beforehand. I may perpetrate the worst.
I can, I will do so!

MARY. But it is dreadful!

MORTIMER. And should I be obliged to kill the Queen,

I've sworn upon the Host it shall be done!

MARY. No, Mortimer, ere so much blood for me——

MORTIMER. What is the life of all compared to you
And to my love? The bond that holds the world
Together may be loosed, a second deluge
Come rolling on and swallow all creation;
Henceforth I value nothing. Ere I quit
My hold on you, may earth and time be ended!

MARY, *retiring*. You frighten me!

MORTIMER, *with unsteady looks, expressive of quiet madness.*
                         Life's but a moment. Death's
But a moment. Let them drag me to Tyburn,
Tear me limb from limb with red-hot pincers——
Violently approaching her with his arms extended.

—If only I can hold you in my arms!

MARY. Madman, stand back!

MORTIMER.   To rest upon this bosom,
To press upon this passion-breathing mouth——

MARY. Leave me, for God's sake, sir! Let me go in——

MORTIMER. I will deliver you: What though it cost
A thousand lives, I'll do it. But I swear,
As God's in heaven, I will possess you too!

MARY. Do hate and love conspire alike to fright me?

MORTIMER. Yes, glowing as their hatred is my love!
They would behead you, they would wound this neck,
So dazzling white, with the disgraceful axe!
Then offer to the living god of joy
What you would sacrifice to bloody hate!

MARY. My woe, my sufferings should be sacred to you!

MORTIMER. The crown is fallen from your brows, O Queen.
Your moving form alone remains, the high,
The godlike influence of your heavenly beauty.
This bids me venture all, this arms my hand
With might and drives me towards the headsman's axe!

MARY. Will no one save me from his raging madness?

MORTIMER. Why shed their blood the daring? Is not life
Life's highest good? And he a madman who

Casts life away? First will I rest my head
Upon the breast that glows with love's own fire!
He presses her violently to his bosom.

MARY. Must I then call for help against the man
Who would deliver me?

MORTIMER. You're not unfeeling!
You made the minstrel Rizzio blest and gave
Yourself a willing prey to Bothwell's arms.

MARY. Presumptuous man!

MORTIMER. *He* was indeed your tyrant.
Well, then—if only terror can obtain you—
By the infernal gods!——

MARY. Away—— You're mad!

MORTIMER. I'll teach you now to tremble before me!

KENNEDY, *entering suddenly.*
They're coming—they approach—the park is filled
With men in arms.

MARY *flies towards the house,* KENNEDY *following.*

MORTIMER, *starting, and catching at his sword.*
I will defend you—I——

SCENE 7

MORTIMER. PAULET *and* DRURY *rush in, in the greatest consternation.* ATTENDANTS *hasten over the stage.*

PAULET. Shut all the portals—draw the bridges up——

MORTIMER. What is the matter, Uncle?

PAULET. Where is the murderess?

MORTIMER. What is the matter? What has passed?

PAULET. The Queen!

MORTIMER. The Queen! What Queen?

PAULET. What Queen? The Queen of England!
She has been murdered on the road to London.
Hastens into the house.

SCENE 8

MORTIMER. *Soon after,* O'KELLY

MORTIMER, *after a pause.*
  Am I then mad? Came not one running by
  But now and cried aloud: "The Queen is murdered!"
  O'Kelly! Comrade——

O'KELLY, *rushing in.*   Flee, our cause is lost!

MORTIMER. What's this? What—lost?

O'KELLY.   Stand not on question. Think
  On speedy flight.

MORTIMER.   What has occurred?

O'KELLY.   That madman
  Sauvage struck at the Queen!

MORTIMER.   Then it is true?

O'KELLY. True, true! Go save yourself!

MORTIMER, *exultingly.*   The Queen is murdered
  And Mary shall ascend the English throne!

O'KELLY. Is murdered? Who said so?

MORTIMER.   Yourself.

O'KELLY.   She lives!
  And I and you and all of us are lost!

MORTIMER. She lives!

O'KELLY.   The blow was badly aimed. Her cloak
  Received it. Shrewsbury disarmed the murderer.

MORTIMER. She lives!

O'KELLY.   She lives to whelm us all in ruin.
  Come! They surround the park——

MORTIMER.   And it was one of
  Our number did this deed!

O'KELLY.   Sauvage, the monk
  From Toulon, whom you saw immersed in thought
  As in the chapel the Pope's bull was read

Which poured anathemas on England's Queen.
He wished to take the nearest, shortest way
To free with one bold stroke the church of God.
He struck the blow upon the road to London.

MORTIMER, *after a long silence.*

Unhappy Mary! Now your death is fixed.
Your very angel has prepared your fall.

O'KELLY. Whither will you take your flight, sir? I go
To hide me in the forests of the north.

MORTIMER. I will remain and still attempt to save
My Queen. If not, my bed shall be her grave.

Exeunt at different sides.

ACT IV

SCENE 1

LONDON. AN ANTECHAMBER IN THE PALACE OF WESTMINSTER

COUNT AUBESPINE, *the* EARLS OF KENT *and* LEICESTER

AUBESPINE. How did it happen? Was it possible
That in the midst of this most loyal people——

LEICESTER. The deed was not attempted by the people.
The assassin was a subject of your King,
A Frenchman.

AUBESPINE.   Sure a lunatic.

LEICESTER.   A Papist,
Count Aubespine.

SCENE 2

Enter BURLEIGH *in conversation with* DAVISON.

BURLEIGH.   Sir, let the death warrant
Be instantly made out, and pass the seal.
The Queen must sign it.

DAVISON.   Sir, it shall be done.
Exit.

AUBESPINE. Praised be almighty Heaven that has averted
Assassination from our much-loved Queen!

BURLEIGH. Praised be His name, who thus has turned to scorn
The malice of our foes!

AUBESPINE.   May Heaven confound
The perpetrator of this cursèd deed!

BURLEIGH. Its perpetrator and its base contriver!

AUBESPINE. Please you, my lord, to bring me to the Queen,
That I may lay the warm congratulations
Of my imperial master at her feet.

BURLEIGH. There is no need of this.

AUBESPINE, *officiously*.   My lord of Burleigh,
I know my duty.

BURLEIGH.   Sir, your duty is
To quit this kingdom and without delay.

AUBESPINE, *stepping back with surprise*. What? How is this?

BURLEIGH.   The sacred character
Of an Ambassador to-day protects you,
But not to-morrow.

AUBESPINE.   What's my crime?

BURLEIGH.   Should I
Once name it, there were then no pardon for it.

AUBESPINE. I hope, my lord, my charge's privilege——

BURLEIGH. Screens not a traitor.

LEICESTER *and* KENT.   Traitor! What?

AUBESPINE.   My lord,
Consider well—

BURLEIGH.   Your passport was discovered
In the assassin's pocket.

KENT.   Righteous Heaven!

AUBESPINE. Sir, many passports have been signed by me.
I cannot know the secret thoughts of men.

BURLEIGH. He in your house confessed and was absolved.

AUBESPINE. My house is open——

BURLEIGH.   —to our enemies.

AUBESPINE. My monarch is insulted in my person:
He will annul the marriage contract.

BURLEIGH.   That
My royal mistress has annulled already.
England will not unite herself with France.
My lord of Kent, I give to you the charge
To see Count Aubespine embarked in safety.

The furious populace has stormed his palace
Where a whole arsenal of arms was found.
Should *he* be found, they'll tear him limb from limb.
Conceal him till their fury is abated.

AUBESPINE. I leave a kingdom where they sport with treaties
And trample underfoot the laws of nations.

Exeunt KENT *and* AUBESPINE.

SCENE 3

LEICESTER, BURLEIGH

LEICESTER. And thus you loose, yourself, the knot of union
Which you officiously, uncalled-for, tied!

BURLEIGH. My aim was good, though fate declared against it.
Happy is he who has so fair a conscience!

LEICESTER. Now you are in your element, my lord.
A monstrous outrage has been just committed,
And darkness veils, as yet, its perpetrators.
Now will a court of inquisition rise;
Each word, each look be weighed; men's very thoughts
Be summoned to the bar. You are, my lord,
The mighty man, the Atlas of the state!

BURLEIGH. In you, my lord, I recognise my master,
For such a victory as your eloquence
Has gained I cannot boast.

LEICESTER.   What means your lordship?

BURLEIGH. You were the man who knew, behind my back,
To lure the Queen to Fotheringay Castle.

LEICESTER. Behind your back! When did I fear to act
Before your face?

BURLEIGH.   *You* led Her Majesty?
Oh no, *you* led her not—it was the Queen
Who was so gracious as to lead *you* thither——

LEICESTER. What do you mean, my lord, by that?

BURLEIGH.   The noble part

You forced the Queen to play! The glorious triumph
Which you prepared for her! Too gracious princess,
So shamelessly, so wantonly to mock
Your unsuspecting goodness, to betray you
So pitiless to your exulting foe!
This is the magnanimity, the grace
Which suddenly possessed you in the council!
The Stuart is for *this* so despicable,
So weak an enemy, that it would scarce
Be worth the pains to stain us with her blood!

LEICESTER. Unworthy wretch! This instant follow me
And answer at the throne your insolence!

BURLEIGH. You'll find me there, my lord, and look you well,
That now your eloquence desert you not!
Exit.

SCENE 4

LEICESTER, *alone; then* MORTIMER

LEICESTER. I am detected. All my plot's disclosed.
Alas, if he has proofs, if she should learn
That I have held a secret correspondence
With her worst enemy, how criminal
Shall I appear to her! How false will then
My counsel seem, and all the fatal pains
I took to lure the Queen to Fotheringay!
I've shamefully betrayed, I have exposed her
To her detested enemy's revilings!
All will appear as if premeditated.
The bitter turn of this sad interview,
The triumph and the tauntings of her rival,
Yes, even the murderous hand, which had prepared
A bloody, monstrous, unexpected fate,
All, all will be ascribed to my suggestions!

MORTIMER *enters, in the most violent uneasiness, and looks
with apprehension round him.*

MORTIMER. My lord! Are we alone?

LEICESTER.   What seek you here?

MORTIMER. Be vigilant.

LEICESTER.   Get you away!

MORTIMER.   They know
That private conferences have been held
At Aubespine's——

LEICESTER.   What's that to me?

MORTIMER.   They know too
That the assassin——

LEICESTER.   That is your affair——
Audacious wretch! To dare to mix my name
In your detested outrage. Go! Defend
Your bloody deeds yourself!

MORTIMER.   But only hear me.

LEICESTER, *violently enraged.*
I know you not—I make no common cause
With murderers!

MORTIMER.   You will not hear me then.
I came to warn you: you too are detected.

LEICESTER. What?

MORTIMER.   Lord Burleigh went to Fotheringay
Just as the luckless deed had been attempted,
Searched with strict scrutiny the Queen's apartments,
And found there——

LEICESTER.   What?

MORTIMER.   A letter which the Queen
Had just addressed to you——

LEICESTER.   Unhappy woman!

MORTIMER. In which she calls on you to keep your word,
Renews the promise of her hand, and mentions
The picture which she sent you.

LEICESTER.   Death and hell!

MORTIMER. Lord Burleigh has the letter.

LEICESTER.   I am lost!

During the following speech of MORTIMER, LEICESTER *goes up and down, as in despair.*

MORTIMER. Improve the moment. Be beforehand with him,
And save yourself—save her! An oath can clear
Your fame: contrive excuses to avert
The worst. *I* am disarmed, can do no more.
My comrades are dispersed—to pieces fallen
Our whole confederacy. For Scotland I,
To rally such new friends as there I may.
'Tis now your turn, my lord.

LEICESTER *stops suddenly, as if resolved.* Sir, you are right.
Goes to the door, opens it, and calls.

Who waits without? Guards! Seize this wretched traitor——
To the OFFICER, *who comes in with* SOLDIERS.

—And guard him closely! A most dreadful plot
Is brought to light. I'll to Her Majesty.

MORTIMER *stands for a time petrified with wonder; collects himself soon; and follows* LEICESTER *with his looks expressive of the most sovereign contempt.*
Over my head he strides. Upon my fall
He builds the bridge of safety. Be it so.
I would not join you, no, even in death.
Life is all a scoundrel has—then keep it!

To the OFFICER OF THE GUARD, *who steps forward to seize him.*

What will you, slave of tyranny, with me?
I laugh to scorn your threatenings: I am free.
Drawing a dagger.

OFFICER. He's armed! Rush in!
They rush upon him; he defends himself.

MORTIMER, *raising his voice.* Curse and destruction
Light on you all! You have betrayed your faith,
Your God, and your true sovereign, and, false
Both to the earthly Mary and the heavenly,
Sell yourselves to a bastard!

OFFICER.   Forward! Seize him!

MORTIMER. Belovèd Queen, I could not set you free.
Yet take a lesson from me how to die.

Mary, Thou holy one, O pray for me
And take me to Thy heavenly home on high!

Stabs himself and falls into the arms of the GUARD.

SCENE 5

THE APARTMENT OF
QUEEN ELIZABETH IN THE
PALACE OF WESTMINSTER

ELIZABETH, *with a letter in her hand;* BURLEIGH

ELIZABETH. The traitor! Thus to lead me, as in triumph,
Into the presence of his paramour!

BURLEIGH. I cannot yet conceive what potent means,
What magic he exerted, to surprise
The prudence of my Queen.

ELIZABETH.   I die for shame!
I thought to humble her and was myself
The object of her bitter scorn!

BURLEIGH.   By this
You see how faithfully I counselled you.

ELIZABETH. Yes, I am sorely punished, that I turned
My ear from your wise counsels; yet I thought
I might confide in him. Who could suspect,
Beneath the vows of faithfullest devotion,
A deadly snare? Leicester, whom I have made
The greatest of the great and in this Court
Allowed to play the master and the king!

BURLEIGH. Yet in that very moment he betrayed you.

ELIZABETH. Now shall she pay me for it with her life!
Is the death warrant there?

BURLEIGH.   It is prepared
As you commanded.

ELIZABETH.   She shall surely die.
He shall behold her fall and fall himself.

Conduct him to the Tower and let him feel
In its full weight the rigour of the law.

BURLEIGH. But he will seek your presence; he will clear——

ELIZABETH. How can he clear himself? Does not the letter
Convict him? All his crimes are manifest!

BURLEIGH. But you are mild and gracious! His appearance——

ELIZABETH. I will never see him. Are orders given,
Not to admit him, should he come?

BURLEIGH.   They are.

PAGE, *entering*. The Earl of Leicester!

ELIZABETH.   The presumptuous man!
I will not see him. Tell him that I will not.

PAGE. I am afraid to bring my lord this message,
Nor would he credit it.

ELIZABETH.   And I have raised him
So high that my own servants tremble more
At him than me!

BURLEIGH, *to the* PAGE. The Queen forbids his presence.

The PAGE *retires slowly.*

ELIZABETH, *after a pause.*
And yet, and yet, might it not be a snare
Laid by the cunning Scot to sever me
From my best friend? The ever-treacherous harlot,
She might have writ the letter just to ruin
The man she hates.

BURLEIGH.   No, gracious Queen, consider——

SCENE 6

LEICESTER *bursts open the door and enters with an imperious
air.*

LEICESTER. Forbid me the apartments of my Queen!

ELIZABETH, *avoiding his sight*. Audacious slave!

LEICESTER.   To turn me from the door!

If for a Burleigh she be visible
She must be so for me!

BURLEIGH.   My lord, you are
Too bold, without permission to intrude——

LEICESTER. My lord, you are too arrogant, to take
The lead in these apartments. What? Permission?

Humbly approaching ELIZABETH.

'Tis from my Sovereign's lips alone that I——

ELIZABETH, *without looking at him.*
Out of my sight, deceitful, worthless traitor!

LEICESTER. You have lent him your ear. I ask the like.

ELIZABETH. Speak, shameless wretch! Increase your crime—
deny it——

LEICESTER. Dismiss this troublesome intruder first.
Retire——!

ELIZABETH, *to* BURLEIGH. Remain, my lord; 'tis my command.

LEICESTER. What has a third to do 'twixt you and me?
I have to clear myself before my Queen,
And I insist upon it that my lord
Retire.

ELIZABETH. This haughty tone befits you well.

LEICESTER. Am not I the man to whom your favour
Has given the highest station? Then what
Your favour gave, by heavens I will maintain!

ELIZABETH. Think not with cunning words to hide the truth.

To BURLEIGH.

My lord, produce the letter.

BURLEIGH.   Here it is.

LEICESTER, *running over the letter without losing his presence
of mind.* It is the Stuart's hand——

ELIZABETH.   Read it, Lord Leicester.

LEICESTER, *having read it quietly.*
I will not by appearances be judged.

ELIZABETH. Can you deny your secret correspondence
With Mary? That *she* sent and *you* received
Her picture? That you gave her hopes?

LEICESTER. I confess
That she hath said the truth.

ELIZABETH. Well then! You wretch!

BURLEIGH. His own words sentence him——

ELIZABETH. Out of my sight!
Away! Conduct the traitor to the Tower!

LEICESTER. I am no traitor; it was wrong, I own,
To make a secret of this step to you.
Yet pure was my intention. It was done
To search into her plots and to confound them.

ELIZABETH. Vain subterfuge!

BURLEIGH. And do you think, my lord——

LEICESTER. I've played a dangerous game. I know it well.
And none but Leicester dare be bold enough
To risk it at this court. The world must know
How I detest this Stuart while my rank
Must sure suffice to——

BURLEIGH. If the course was good,
Wherefore conceal it?

LEICESTER. You are used, my lord,
To prate before you act. That is your manner.
But mine is first to act and then to speak.

BURLEIGH. Ay, now you speak—because you must.

LEICESTER, *measuring him proudly and disdainfully with his
eyes.* And *you*
Boast of a wonderful, a mighty action,
That *you* have saved the Queen, have snatched away
The mask from treachery. All is known to *you*.
And yet despite your cunning, Mary Stuart
Was free today, had *I* not hindered it!

BURLEIGH. *You*, sir?

LEICESTER. Yes, *I*, my lord. The Queen confided
In Mortimer: she opened to the youth
Her inmost soul. Yes, she went farther still:
She gave him too a secret bloody charge.
Say, is it so, or not?

The QUEEN *and* BURLEIGH *look at one another with astonishment.*

BURLEIGH.   Whence know you this?

LEICESTER. And where, my lord, where were your thousand eyes,
Not to discover Mortimer was false?
That he, the Guise's tool, a raging Papist,
Was come to free the Stuart and to murder
The Queen of England!

ELIZABETH, *with the utmost astonishment.*
                         Edward Mortimer?

LEICESTER. This very day she was to have been torn
From her confinement. He this very moment
Disclosed his plan to me. I took him prisoner
And gave him to the guard, when in despair
He slew himself.

ELIZABETH.   Mortimer! I have been
Deceived beyond example! Mortimer!

BURLEIGH. This happened then but now? Since last we parted?

LEICESTER. For my own sake I must lament the deed—
That he was thus cut off. His testimony,
Were he alive, had fully cleared my name.
I was surrendering him to open justice
To verify and fix my innocence
Before the world.

BURLEIGH.   He killed himself, you say.
Is it so? Or did *you* kill him?

LEICESTER *goes to the door and calls.* Officer!

Enter the OFFICER OF THE GUARD.

Sir, tell the Queen how Mortimer expired.

OFFICER. I was on duty in the palace porch
When suddenly my lord threw wide the door
And ordered me to take the knight in charge,
Denouncing him a traitor. Mortimer
Straight drew a dagger out and plunged the steel
Into his heart.

The OFFICER *withdraws.*

ELIZABETH.   Abyss beneath abyss
Of monstrous deeds!

LEICESTER.   Who was it then, my Queen,
Who saved you? Was it Burleigh?

BURLEIGH.   Mortimer
Died most conveniently for *you,* my lord.

ELIZABETH. What I should say I know not. I believe you
And I believe you not. A curse on her
Who caused me all this anguish!

LEICESTER.   She must die.
I formerly advised you to suspend
The sentence till some arm was raised anew
On her behalf; and now the case has happened.

BURLEIGH. You give this counsel? You?

LEICESTER.   However it wound
My feelings to be forced to this extreme,
Yet now I see most clearly, now I *feel*
That the Queen's welfare asks this bloody victim.

BURLEIGH, *to the* QUEEN.
Since then his lordship shows such earnest zeal,
Such loyalty, 'twere well, were he appointed,
To see to the execution of the sentence.

LEICESTER. Who? I?

BURLEIGH.   Yes, you. You surely could not find
A better means to shake off the suspicion
Which rests upon you still than to command
Her, whom 'tis said you love, to be beheaded.

ELIZABETH, *looking steadfastly at* LEICESTER.
My lord advises well. So be it, then!

LEICESTER. A man who stands so near the royal person
Should have no knowledge of such fatal scenes;
But yet, to prove my zeal to satisfy
My Queen, I waive my charge's privilege.

ELIZABETH. Lord Burleigh shall partake this duty with you.

To BURLEIGH.

So: be the warrant instantly prepared.

BURLEIGH *withdraws. A tumult heard without.*

SCENE 7

Enter the EARL OF KENT

ELIZABETH. How now, my lord of Kent? What uproar's this
I hear without?

KENT.   My Queen, it is your people,
Who, round the palace ranged, impatiently
Demand to see their sovereign.

ELIZABETH.   What's their wish?

KENT. A panic terror has already spread
Through London that your life has been attempted;
That murderers commissioned from the Pope
Beset you; that the Catholics have sworn
To rescue from her prison Mary Stuart,
And to proclaim her Queen. Your loyal people
Believe it and are mad. They want her head.

ELIZABETH. What? Will they force me then?

KENT.   They are resolved——

SCENE 8

Enter BURLEIGH *and* DAVISON, *with a paper.*

ELIZABETH. Well, Davison?

DAVISON *approaches earnestly.* Your orders are obeyed,
My Queen——

ELIZABETH.   What orders, sir?

*As she is about to take the paper, she shudders and starts
back.*

                    Alas!

BURLEIGH.   Obey
Your people's voice: it is the voice of God.

ELIZABETH. But who will give me the assurance, sir,

That what I now hear *is* the people's voice?
If I should listen to this multitude
Do I not have to fear a different voice
Will soon be heard, a different multitude?
And that the men who force me to this step
Will heavily condemn me when 'tis taken?

SCENE 9

Enter the EARL OF SHREWSBURY, *with great emotion.*

SHREWSBURY. Hold fast, my Queen, they wish to hurry you.

Seeing DAVISON *with the paper.*

Or is it then decided?

ELIZABETH.   I'm constrained——

SHREWSBURY. Who can constrain *you?* You are Queen of
      England.
  Here must your majesty assert its rights:
  Command those savage voices to be silent
  Who take upon themselves to put constraint
  Upon your royal will and rule your judgement.

BURLEIGH. Judgement has long been passed. It is not now
  The time to pass, but execute the sentence.

KENT, *who, on* SHREWSBURY's *entry, had retired, comes back.*
  The tumult gains apace. There are no means
  To moderate the people.

ELIZABETH, *to* SHREWSBURY. See, my lord,
  How they press on.

SHREWSBURY.   I only ask a respite.
  A single word traced by your hand decides
  The peace, the happiness of all your life.
  Wait for a moment of tranquillity.

BURLEIGH, *violently.*
  Wait for it—pause—delay—till flames of fire
  Consume the realm—until the fifth attempt
  At murder be successful! God, indeed,
  Had thrice delivered you. Your late escape

Was marvellous, and to expect again
A miracle would be to tempt the Lord!

SHREWSBURY. Yet think of this. You tremble now before
The living Mary: you would tremble more
Before a murdered, a beheaded Mary.
When you have done the bloody deed, *then* go
Through London, seek your people which till now
Delighted swarmed about you: you shall see
Another London and another people.
No more the dignity of godlike justice
Will beam about you. Fear, the dread ally
Of tyranny, will march before you shuddering
And make a wilderness of every street!

ELIZABETH, *after a pause.*
I'm weary of my life and of my crown.
If heaven decree that one of us two Queens
Must perish to secure the other's life—
And sure it must be so—why should not I
Be she who yields? My people must decide:
I give them back the sovereignty they gave.
God is my witness that I have not lived
For my own sake but for my people's welfare.
If they expect from this false, fawning Stuart,
The younger sovereign, more happy days,
I will descend with pleasure from the throne
And back repair to Woodstock's quiet bowers
Where once I spent my unambitious youth
And far removed from all the vanities
Of earthly power found within myself
True majesty. I am not made to rule—

BURLEIGH. You say you love your people above yourself:
Then prove it. Choose not peace for your own heart
And leave your kingdom to the storms of discord.
Think on the church. Shall, with this Papist queen,
The ancient superstition be renewed,
The monk resume his sway, the Roman legate
In pomp march hither, lock our churches up,
Dethrone our monarchs? I demand of you

The souls of all your subjects! As you now
Shall act, they all are saved or all are lost!
A pause.

ELIZABETH. I would be left alone. I'll lay my doubts
Before the Judge of all. I am resolved
To act as He shall teach. Withdraw, my lords.
To DAVISON, *who lays the paper on the table.*
You, sir, remain in waiting, close at hand.

The LORDS *withdraw.* SHREWSBURY *alone stands for a few moments before the* QUEEN, *regards her significantly, then withdraws slowly and with an expression of the deepest anguish.*

SCENE 10

ELIZABETH, *alone*

ELIZABETH. O servitude of popularity!
Disgraceful slavery! How weary am I
Of flattering this idol which my soul
Despises in its inmost depth! O when
Shall I once more be free upon this throne?
I must respect the people's voice and strive
To win the favour of the multitude
And please the fancies of a mob, whom nought
But jugglers' tricks delight. Do not call him
A king, who needs must please the world about him.
But have I practised justice all my life
Only to bind my hands against this first
Unavoidable act of violence?
Had I but been a tyrant, like my sister,
My predecessor, I could fearless then
Have shed this royal blood, but am I now
Just by my own free choice? No, I am forced
By stern necessity to use this virtue,
Necessity which binds even monarchs' wills.
Surrounded by my foes, my people's love

Alone supports me on my envied throne.
All Europe's powers confederate to attack me;
The Pope declares me excommunicate;
While France betrays me with a kiss; and Spain
Prepares a great Armada to destroy me.
Thus stand I in contention with the world,
A poor defenceless woman. I must now
Remove the stain in my imperial birth
By which my father cast disgrace upon me.
In vain with princely virtues would I hide it:
My enemies uncover it again.

Walking up and down, with quick and agitated steps.

The hated name of every ill I feel
Is Mary Stuart. Were she but no more
On earth, I should be free as mountain air.

Standing still.

With what disdain did she look down on me!

Advancing to the table hastily and taking the pen.

I am a bastard, am I? Hapless wretch,
Your death will make my birth legitimate.

*She signs with resolution; then lets her pen fall: and steps
back with an expression of terror. After a pause, she rings.*

SCENE 11

ELIZABETH, DAVISON

ELIZABETH. Where are their lordships?

DAVISON.   They are gone to quell
The tumult of the people. The alarm
Was instantly appeased when they beheld
The Earl of Shrewsbury. "That's he!" exclaimed
A hundred voices. "That's the man—he saved
The Queen. Hear *him*—the bravest man in England!"
And now began the gallant Talbot, blamed
In gentle words the people's violence
And used such strong, persuasive eloquence

That all were pacified and silently
They slunk away.

ELIZABETH.   The fickle multitude!
Which turns with every wind. Unhappy he
Who leans upon this reed!

As he is going towards the door.

                    And, sir, this paper,
Receive it back; I place it in your hands.

DAVISON *casts a look upon the paper and starts back.*
My gracious Queen—your name! 'Tis then decided.

ELIZABETH. I had but to subscribe it—I have done so—
A paper sure cannot decide—a name
Kills not——

DAVISON.   Your name, my Queen, beneath this paper
Is most decisive—kills. This fatal scroll
Commands the Sheriff and Commissioners
To take departure straight for Fotheringay
And to the Queen of Scots announce her death
Which must at dawn be put in execution.
As soon as I have parted with this writ
Her race is run——

ELIZABETH.   Yes, sir, the Lord has placed
This weighty business in your feeble hands;
Seek Him in prayer, to light you with His wisdom.
I go, and leave you, sir, to do your duty.
Going.

DAVISON. But leave me not till I have heard your will.
Say, have you placed this warrant in my hands
To see that it be speedily enforced?

ELIZABETH. That you must do, as your own prudence dictates.

DAVISON, *interrupting her quickly, and alarmed.*
Permit me, in this weighty act, to be
Your passive instrument, without a will.
Tell me in plain undoubted terms your pleasure.

ELIZABETH. Its name declares its meaning.

DAVISON.   Do you, then,
My liege, command its instant execution?

ELIZABETH. I said not that; I tremble but to think it.

DAVISON. Shall I retain it, then, till further orders?

ELIZABETH. At your own risk; you answer the event.

DAVISON. I! Gracious Heavens!—— O speak, my Queen, your
    pleasure!

ELIZABETH. My pleasure is that this unhappy business
  Be no more mentioned to me! That at last
  I may be freed from it, and that forever!

DAVISON. What shall I do with this mysterious scroll?

ELIZABETH. I have declared it. Plague me, sir, no longer.

DAVISON. You have declared it, say you? But, my Queen,
  You have said nothing——

ELIZABETH *stamps on the ground.* Insupportable!
  Exit.

SCENE 12

DAVISON, *then* BURLEIGH

DAVISON. She goes. She leaves me. How to act I know not.
  Should I retain it? Should I forward it?
  To BURLEIGH, *who enters.*
  Oh, I am glad that you are come, my lord.

BURLEIGH. The Queen was with you.

DAVISON.   She has quitted me
  In bitter anger. Pray advise me, help me,
  Save me from this fell agony of doubt.
  My lord, here is the warrant: it is signed.

BURLEIGH. Indeed? Indeed? Then give it me!

DAVISON.   I may not.

BURLEIGH. What?

DAVISON.   She has not yet explained her final will.

BURLEIGH. Explained! She has subscribed it. Give it me.

DAVISON. I am to execute it and I am not.

Great Heavens, I know not what I am to do!

BURLEIGH, *urging more violently*

It must be now, this moment, executed—
The warrant, sir. You're lost if you delay.

DAVISON. So am I also if I act too rashly.

BURLEIGH. What strange infatuation! Give it me!

Snatches the paper from him, and exit with it.

DAVISON. What would you? Stop! You will be my destruction!

ACT V

SCENE 1

THE SCENE IS THE SAME AS IN ACT I

HANNAH KENNEDY, *in deep mourning, her eyes still red from weeping, in great but quiet anguish is employed in sealing letters and parcels. Her sorrow often interrupts her occupation, and she is seen at such intervals to pray in silence.* PAULET, *also in mourning, enters, followed by many* SERVANTS, *who bear golden and silver vessels, mirrors, paintings, and other valuables, and fill the back part of the stage with them.* PAULET *delivers to the* NURSE *a box of jewels and a paper and seems to inform her by signs that it contains the inventory of the effects the Queen had brought with her. At the sight of these riches, the anguish of the* NURSE *is renewed. She sinks into a deep melancholy, during which* PAULET *and the* SERVANTS *silently retire.*

MELVIL *enters*

KENNEDY *screams as soon as she observes him.*
Melvil! Can it be you I see again?

MELVIL. Yes, faithful Kennedy, we meet once more.

KENNEDY. You come——?

MELVIL. To take an everlasting leave.

KENNEDY. And now at length, now on the fatal morn
Which brings her death, they grant our royal lady
The presence of her friends.

MELVIL. Restrain your grief,
And when the rest give way to tears we two
Will lead her with heroic resolution
And be her staff upon the road to death!

KENNEDY. Melvil, you are deceived if you suppose
The Queen has need of our support to meet

Her death with firmness. She it is, my friend,
Who will exhibit the undaunted heart.

MELVIL. Received she firmly, then, the sad decree
Of death? 'Tis said that she was not prepared.

KENNEDY. Freedom was promised us. This very night
Had Mortimer engaged to bear us hence.
And thus the Queen, perplexed 'twixt hope and fear,
Sat waiting for the morning. On a sudden
Our ears are startled by repeated blows
Of many hammers, and we think we hear
The approach of our deliverers. Then suddenly
The portals are thrown open. It is Paulet
Who comes to tell us that the carpenters
Erect beneath our feet the murderous scaffold.
She turns aside, overpowered by anguish.

MELVIL. How bore the Queen this terrible affliction?

KENNEDY, *after a pause in which she has somewhat collected
herself.* Not by degrees can we relinquish life.
Quick, sudden, in the twinkling of an eye
The separation must be made, and God
Imparted to our mistress at that moment
His grace, to cast away each earthly hope
And, firm and full of faith, to mount the skies.

MELVIL. Where is she now? Can you not lead me to her?

KENNEDY. She spent the last remainder of the night
In prayer, and from her dearest friends she took
Her last farewell in writing. Then she wrote
Her will with her own hand.

MELVIL.   Who attends her?

KENNEDY. None but her women and physician Burgoyne.

SCENE 2

Enter MARGARET CURL.

KENNEDY. How, madam, fares the Queen? Is she awake?

MARGARET CURL, *drying her tears.*
She is already dressed—she asks for you.

KENNEDY, *to* MELVIL, *who seems to wish to accompany her.*
Follow me not, good Melvil, till the Queen
Has been prepared to see you.

Exit.

MARGARET CURL.   Melvil? You're
The ancient steward?

MELVIL.   Yes.

MARGARET CURL.   My name is Curl.

A pause.

You come from London, sir. Can you give me
No tidings of my husband?

MELVIL.   It is said
He will be set at liberty as soon——

MARGARET CURL. As soon as our dear Queen shall be no more!
He is our lady's murderer. They say
It was his testimony which condemned her.

MELVIL. That is so.

MARGARET CURL. Curse him! He has borne false witness!

MELVIL. Think, madam, what you say.

MARGARET CURL.   I will maintain it
With every sacred oath before the court!
I will repeat it in his face! I say
That she dies innocent!

MELVIL.   God grant it true!

SCENE 3

Enter BURGOYNE, *followed by* HANNAH KENNEDY.

BURGOYNE. Melvil!

MELVIL.   Burgoyne!

They silently embrace.

BURGOYNE, *to* MARGARET CURL. Go fetch a cup of wine.
'Tis for our lady.

Exit MARGARET CURL.

MELVIL. Is Queen Mary sick?

BURGOYNE. Deceived by the sublimity of courage
She thinks she has no need of nourishment.
I would not give her enemies that triumph
To say that it was fear that blanched her cheek.

MELVIL. May I approach her now?

KENNEDY. She'll come herself.

SCENE 4

Enter two WOMEN OF THE CHAMBER *weeping, and in deep mourning.*

FIRST WOMAN. She has sent us from her——

SECOND WOMAN. Bade us leave her
Alone. She is communing with her God.

SCENE 5

Enter MARGARET CURL, *bearing a golden cup of wine. She places it hastily upon the table and leans, pale and trembling, against a chair.*

MELVIL. How, madam? What has frightened you?

BURGOYNE. Speak, madam!

MARGARET CURL. As I went down the staircase which conducts
To the great hall below, a door stood open——
O Heaven!

MELVIL. What saw you?

MARGARET CURL. All the walls were hung
With black. A spacious scaffold overspread
With sable cloth was raised above the floor,
And in the middle of the scaffold stood
A dreadful sable block. Upon it lay
A naked, polished axe. The hall was full
Of cruel people crowding round the scaffold,

Who, with a horrid thirst for human blood,
Seemed waiting for the victim.

MELVIL.   She approaches.

SCENE 6

Enter MARY *in white and sumptuously arrayed, as for a
festival. She wears, hanging from her neck on a row of small
beads, an Agnus Dei; a rosary hangs from her girdle; she
bears a crucifix in her hand and a diadem of precious stones
binds her hair; her large black veil is thrown back. On her
entrance, all present fall back on both sides with the most
violent expressions of anguish.* MELVIL *falls involuntarily
upon his knees.*

MARY, *with quiet majesty, looking round the whole circle.*
Why these complaints? Why do you weep? You should
Rejoice with me that now at length the end
Of my long woe approaches; that my shackles
Fall off, my prison opens, and my soul,
Delighted, mounts on seraph's wings and seeks
The land of everlasting liberty.
Then do not weep. Death is a helpful friend.
The foulest criminal's ennobled by his
Sufferings. Now I feel the crown upon
My brows, and dignity possess my soul.

Advancing a few steps.

What? Melvil here? My worthy sir, not so;
Arise. You rather come in time to see
The triumph of your mistress than her death.
How have you fared, sir, in this hostile land?

MELVIL. No other evil galled me but my grief
For you and that I wanted power to serve you.

MARY. Sir, to your loyal bosom I commit
My latest wishes. Bear then, sir, my blessing
To the most Christian king, my royal brother.
I bless the Cardinal, my honoured uncle.
I bless the Holy Father, the Vicegerent

Of Christ on earth, who will, I trust, bless me.
They are remembered in my will, good Melvil.
Turning to her servants.

I have bequeathed you to my royal brother
Of France who will give you another home.
Swear by this image of our suffering Lord
To leave this fatal land when I'm no more.

MELVIL, *touching the crucifix.*

I swear obedience in the name of all.

MARY. What I still possess be shared among you,
And what I wear upon the way to death!

To the LADIES OF HER CHAMBER.

To Alice, Gertrude, Rosamund, I leave
My clothes, my pearls, my trinkets. Margaret,
That I have not avenged your husband's fault
On you I hope my legacy will prove.
My memory will be to you, my Hannah,
The dearest jewel. Take this handkerchief.
I worked it for you, Hannah. You will bind
My eyes with it when it is time. Now come!

She stretches forth her hands; the women violently weeping, fall successively at her feet, and kiss her outstretched hand.

Margaret, farewell. My Alice, fare thee well.
Thanks, Burgoyne, for your honest faithful service.
Gertrude, your lips are hot. I too was loved.
May a deserving husband bless my Gertrude!
Bertha, you have made the better choice of heaven.
So haste you to fulfil your vows. The goods
Of earth are all deceitful. You may learn
This lesson from your Queen. No more. Farewell,
Farewell, farewell, my friends, farewell forever.

She turns suddenly from them; all but MELVIL *retire at different sides.*

SCENE 7

MARY, MELVIL

MARY, *after the others are all gone.*
   Melvil, one thought alone there is which binds
   My troubled soul nor suffers it to fly
   Delighted and at liberty to heaven.

MELVIL. Disclose it to me. Ease your bosom, madam.

MARY. A priest of my religion is denied me.
   And I disdain to take the sacrament
   From priests of a false faith. I die believing
   In my own church, for she alone can save.

MELVIL. Compose your heart. The fervent, pious wish
   Is prized in heaven as high as the performance.
   The word is dead. 'Tis faith which brings to life.

MARY. Our faith must have some earthly pledge to ground
   Its claims to the high bliss of heaven. For this
   Our God became incarnate and inclosed
   Mysteriously his unseen heavenly grace
   Within the outward figure of a body.
   Ah, happy they, who for the glad communion
   Of pious prayer, meet in the house of God!
   The altar is adorned, the tapers blaze,
   The bell invites, the incense soars on high,
   The bishop stands enrobed, he takes the cup
   And, blessing it, declares the mystery,
   The transformation of the elements,
   While the believing people fall delighted
   To worship and adore the present Godhead.
   Alas, that I should be debarred from this.

MELVIL. The withered staff can send forth verdant branches,
   And he who from the rock called living water
   Can change——
   Seizing the cup, which stands upon the table.
         —the earthly contents of this cup

Into a substance of celestial grace!

MARY. Melvil! Oh yes, I understand you, Melvil!
Here is no priest, no church, no sacrament.
But the Redeemer says: "When two or three
Are in my name assembled, I am with them."

MELVIL. You err. Here *is* a priest—here *is* a God.
A God descends to you in real presence.

*At these words he uncovers his tonsured head and shows a
Host in a golden vessel.*

I am a priest, O Queen, I have received
Upon my head the seven consecrations.
I bring you from His Holiness this Host
Which he himself has deigned to bless for you.

MARY. As an immortal one on golden clouds
Descends, as once the angel from on high
Delivered the Apostle from his fetters—
He scorns all bars, he scorns the soldier's sword,
He steps undaunted through the bolted portals,
And fills the dungeon with his native glory—
So here the messenger of heaven appears
When every earthly champion had deceived me.

She sinks before him on her knees.

MELVIL, *making over her the sign of the cross.*
Hear, Mary Queen of Scotland. In the name
Of God the Father, Son, and Holy Ghost,
Do you swear in your confession here before me
To speak the truth before the God of truth?

MARY. Before my God and you my heart lies open.

MELVIL. Declare the sin which weighs so heavily
Upon your conscience since your last confession.

MARY. I hope forgiveness of my sins from God,
Yet could I not forgive my enemy.

MELVIL. Do you repent the sin? Are you, in sooth,
Resolved to leave this world at peace with all?

MARY. As surely as I wish the joys of heaven.

MELVIL. What other sin has armed your heart against you?

MARY. My heart was vainly turned towards the man
Who left me in misfortune, who deceived me.

MELVIL. Do you repent the sin? And have you turned
Your heart from this idolatry to God?

MARY. It was the hardest trial I have passed:
This last of earthly bonds is torn asunder.

MELVIL. What other sin disturbs your guilty conscience?

MARY. By my connivance fell the King, my husband.
I gave my hand and heart to a seducer.
By rigid penance I have made atonement,
Yet in my soul the worm is gnawing still.

MELVIL. And has your heart no other accusation
Which has not been confessed and washed away?

MARY. You have heard all with which my heart is charged.

MELVIL. Think on the punishments with which the church
Threatens imperfect and reserved confession:
This is the sin to everlasting death.

MARY. I have hid nothing.

MELVIL.   Will you then conceal
From God the crime for which you are condemned?
You tell me nothing of the share you had
In Parry's treason and in Babington's!

MARY. Within the narrow limits of an hour
I shall appear before my Judge's throne:
But, I repeat it, my confession's ended.

MELVIL. Consider well. The heart is a deceiver.
You have perhaps, with sly equivocation,
The *word* avoided which would make you guilty
Although your *will* was party to the crime.

MARY. I swear that, neither by intent nor deed,
Have I attempted my oppressor's life.

MELVIL. Your secretaries must have witnessed falsely!

MARY. It is as I have said. What they have witnessed
The Lord will judge.

MELVIL.   Then, satisfied of your
Own innocence, you mount the fatal scaffold?

MARY. God in his mercy lets me now atone
  My youth's misdeeds by undeservèd death.

MELVIL, *making over her the sign of the cross.*
  Sink a devoted victim on the altar:
  Thus shall your blood atone the blood you spilt.
  And so, by the authority which God
  Hath unto me committed, I absolve you
  From all your sins. Be as your faith your welfare!
  He gives her the Host.
  Receive the body which for you was offered.
  He takes the cup which stands upon the table, consecrates it with silent prayer, then presents it to her.
  Receive the blood which for your sins was shed.
  She takes the cup.
  So may you henceforth, in His realm of joy,
  A fair transfigured spirit, join yourself
  Forever with the Godhead and forever!
  He sets down the cup; hearing a noise, he covers his head and goes to the door; MARY *remains in silent devotion on her knees.* MELVIL, *returning.*
  Have you the strength to smother every impulse
  Of malice and of hate?

MARY.   I have to God
  Devoted both my hatred and my love.

MELVIL. Prepare then to receive my lords of Burleigh
  And of Leicester.

SCENE 8

Enter BURLEIGH, LEICESTER, *and* PAULET. LEICESTER *remains in the background, without raising his eyes;* BURLEIGH, *who remarks his confusion, steps between him and the Queen.*

BURLEIGH.   I come, my Lady Stuart,
  To receive your last commands.

MARY.   Thanks, my lord.

My will declares my last desires on earth:
I've placed it in Sir Amias Paulet's hands
And humbly beg that it may be fulfilled.

PAULET. You may rely on that.

MARY.   I beg that all
My servants unmolested may return
To France or Scotland as their wishes lead.

BURLEIGH. It shall be as you wish.

MARY.   And since my body
Is not to rest in consecrated ground,
I pray you suffer this my faithful servant
To bear my heart to France.

BURLEIGH.   It shall be done.
What wishes else?

MARY.   Unto Her Majesty
Of England bear a sister's salutation.
Tell her I pardon her my death, repent
The passion of my speech to her. God save
The Queen!

BURLEIGH.   You still refuse the dean's assistance?

MARY. My lord, my peace with God is made.

To PAULET.

Good sir,
I have unwittingly caused you much sorrow:
Your nephew was your age's only stay——

PAULET, *giving her his hand.*

Go your way in peace! The Lord be with you!

SCENE 9

HANNAH KENNEDY *and* QUEEN MARY's *other women crowd
into the room with marks of horror. The* SHERIFF *follows
them, a white staff in his hand. Behind are seen, through
the open doors, men under arms.*

MARY. What ails you, Hannah? Yes, my hour is come.

The Sheriff's here to lead me to my fate,
And part we must. Farewell!

KENNEDY *and* MARGARET CURL. We will not leave you!
We will not part from you!

MARY, *to* MELVIL.   You, worthy sir,
And my dear faithful Hannah, shall attend me.

BURLEIGH. For this I have no warrant.

MARY.   How, my lord?

BURLEIGH. 'Tis ordered that no woman shall ascend
The scaffold steps with you. Their tears and moans——

MARY. She bore me on her arms into this life,
Let her then gently lead me to my death.
She shall not weep, my lord, she shall not moan.

PAULET, *to* BURLEIGH. Yield to her wishes.

BURLEIGH.   Be it so.

MARY.   I now
Have nothing in this world to wish for more.
She takes the crucifix and kisses it.

As once Thy arms were stretched upon the cross,
Let them be now extended to receive me!

*She turns round to go. At the same moment her eyes fall
upon* LEICESTER, *who, on her going, starts involuntarily and
turns his eyes towards her. At this sight* MARY *trembles, her
knees fail her, she is about to fall, when* LEICESTER *catches
at her and receives her in his arms. She regards him for
some time earnestly and in silence. He cannot support her
looks. At length she speaks.*

You keep your word, my lord of Leicester. For
You promised me your arm to lead me forth
From prison and you lend it to me now
As now I leave these dismal halls forever.
All is fulfilled, and you have saved your honour.

*He stands as if annihilated; she continues, with a gentle
voice.*

Led by your hand and happy in your love,
I hoped once more to taste the joys of life.
Yes, Leicester, I may venture to confess

Without a blush the frailty I have conquered.
Farewell, my lord, and, if you can, be happy!
To woo two queens has been your daring aim.
You have disdained a tender, loving heart,
Betrayed it, in the hope to win a proud one.
Kneel at the feet of Queen Elizabeth.
May your reward not prove your punishment!
Farewell: I now have nothing more on earth.

She goes, preceded by the SHERIFF, *at her side* MELVIL *and her* NURSE. BURLEIGH *and* PAULET *follow. The others, wailing, follow her with their eyes till she disappears; they then retire through the other two doors.*

SCENE 10

LEICESTER, *remaining alone.*
She's gone, a spirit purged from earthly stain,
And the despair of hell remains for me!
Where is the purpose now with which I came
To see her head descend upon the block
With unaverted and indifferent eyes?
How does her presence wake my slumbering shame?
Must she in death surround me with love's toils?
Lost, wretched man! No more it suits you now
To melt away in womanly compassion!
Pity be dumb! Mine eyes be petrified!
I'll see! I *will* be witness of her fall!

He advances with resolute steps towards the door through which MARY *passed; but stops suddenly halfway.*

I cannot see her die. Hark! What was that?
They are already there. Beneath my feet
The bloody business is preparing. Hark!
I hear their voices. Hence! Away, away!

He attempts to escape by another door, finds it locked, and returns.

How? Does some demon chain me to this spot
To hear what I would shudder to behold?

That voice—it is the dean's, exhorting her—
She interrupts him—— Hark! She prays aloud.
Her voice is firm. Now all is still, quite still,
And sobs and women's moans are all I hear.
Now they undress her—they remove the stool—
She kneels upon the cushion—lays her head——

*Having spoken these last words and paused awhile, he is
seen with a convulsive motion suddenly to shrink and faint
away. A confused hum of voices is heard at the same moment from below and continues for some time.*

SCENE 11

THE APARTMENT OF QUEEN ELIZABETH
(AS IN THE SECOND PART OF ACT IV)

ELIZABETH, *entering from a side door, her gait and action ex-
pressive of the most violent uneasiness.*
No message yet? And no one here? O God,
Will evening never come? Stands the sun still?
Is it accomplished?—— Is it not?—— I shudder
At both events and do not dare to ask.
My lord of Leicester comes not—— Nor Lord Burleigh——
Who's there?

SCENE 12

Enter a PAGE.

ELIZABETH.   Returned alone? Where are the lords?
PAGE. My Lord High Treasurer and the Earl of Leicester——
ELIZABETH. Where are they?
PAGE.   They are not in London.
ELIZABETH.   No?
Where are they then?
PAGE.   That no one could inform me.

Before the dawn, mysteriously, in haste,
They quitted London.

ELIZABETH, *exultingly.* I am Queen of England!

Walking up and down in the greatest agitation.

Go—— Call me—— No, remain, boy! She is dead.
Now have I room upon the earth at last.
Why do I shake? And whence the dread? The grave
Covers my fears. Who dares say I did it?
I have enough tears left to weep her fall.

To the PAGE.

Command my secretary Davison
To come to me this instant. Let the Earl
Of Shrewsbury be called. But here he comes.

Exit PAGE.

SCENE 13

Enter SHREWSBURY.

ELIZABETH. Welcome, my noble lord. What tidings? Speak!

SHREWSBURY. My liege, the doubts that hung upon my heart
Directed me this morning to the Tower,
Where Mary's secretaries, Curl and Nau,
Are now confined as prisoners, for I wished
Once more to put their evidence to proof.
On my arrival the lieutenant seemed
Embarrassed and perplexed; refused to show me
His prisoners. But my threats obtained admittance.
With hair dishevelled, on his pallet lay
This Curl, like one tormented by a fury.
The miserable man no sooner saw me
Than at my feet he fell and there with screams
Implored, conjured me to acquaint him with
His sovereign's destiny, for vague reports
Had somehow reached the dungeons of the Tower
That she had been condemned to suffer death.
When I confirmed these tidings, adding too

That on his evidence she had been doomed,
He started wildly up, caught by the throat
His comrade Nau, with the giant strength
Of madness tore him to the ground and tried
To strangle him. No sooner had we saved
The wretch from his fierce grapple than at once
He turned his rage against himself and beat
His breast with savage fists, and cursed himself.
Curl's evidence was false; the fatal letters
To Babington which he had sworn were true
He now denounced as forgeries. For he
Had set down words the Queen had never spoken;
The traitor Nau had led him to this treason.
Then ran he to the casement, threw it wide
With frantic force, and cried into the street
So loud that all the people gathered round:
"I am the man, Queen Mary's secretary,
The traitor who accused his mistress falsely!
I bore false witness and am cursed forever!"

ELIZABETH. You said yourself that he had lost his wits.
A madman's words prove nothing.

SHREWSBURY.   Yet this madness
Serves in itself to swell the proof. My liege,
Give order for a new inquiry!

ELIZABETH.   Sir,
To set your mind at rest, the inquiry shall
Be straight renewed. Well that 'tis not too late!

SCENE 14

Enter DAVISON.

ELIZABETH. The sentence, sir, which I but late entrusted
Unto your keeping—— Where is it?

DAVISON, *in the utmost astonishment*. The sentence!

ELIZABETH, *more urgent*.
Which yesterday I gave into your charge.

DAVISON. Into my charge, my liege!

ELIZABETH.   The people urged
And baited me to sign it. I perforce
Was driven to yield obedience to their will.
To gain time was my purpose. You remember
What then I told you. Now, the paper, sir!

SHREWSBURY. Restore it, sir, affairs have changed since then.
The inquiry must be set on foot anew.

DAVISON. Anew! Eternal mercy!

ELIZABETH.   Why this pause,
This hesitation? Where, sir, is the paper?

DAVISON. I have it not!

ELIZABETH.   What? What, sir?

SHREWSBURY.   God in heaven!

DAVISON. It is in Burleigh's hands—since yesterday.

ELIZABETH. Did I not lay my strict injunction on you
To keep it carefully?

DAVISON.   No such injunction
Was laid on me, my liege——

ELIZABETH.   Give me the lie?
Opprobrious wretch! When did I order you
To give the paper into Burleigh's hands?

DAVISON. Never, expressly—in so many words——

ELIZABETH. If evil come of this officious deed
Your life shall answer the event to me.
Earl Shrewsbury, you see how my good name
Has been abused.

SHREWSBURY.   I see. Would I did not!

SCENE 15

Enter BURLEIGH.

BURLEIGH, *bowing his knee before the* QUEEN.
Long life and glory to my royal mistress,
And may all enemies of her dominions
End like this Stuart!

SHREWSBURY *hides his face.* DAVISON *wrings his hands in despair.*

ELIZABETH.   Speak, my lord. Did you
From me receive the warrant?

BURLEIGH.   No, my Queen;
From Davison.

ELIZABETH.   And did he in my name
Deliver it?

BURLEIGH.   No, that I cannot say.

ELIZABETH. Just was the sentence; we are free from blame
Before the world. Yet it behoved you not
To intercept our natural clemency.
For this, my lord, I banish you my presence.

Exit BURLEIGH.

To DAVISON.

For, you, sir, who have traitorously betrayed
A sacred pledge entrusted to your care
A more severe tribunal is prepared:
Let him be straight conducted to the Tower,
And capital arraignments filed against him.

DAVISON *is led away.*

My honest Talbot, you alone have proved,
Of all my counsellors, an upright man:
You shall henceforward be my guide, my friend.

SHREWSBURY. Oh, banish not the truest of your friends
Nor cast those into prison who for you
Have acted, who for you are silent now!
And suffer me, great Queen, to give the seal
Which these twelve years I've borne unworthily
Back to your royal hands and take my leave.

ELIZABETH, *surprised.*

No, Shrewsbury. You surely would not now
Desert me? No, not now!

SHREWSBURY.   Pardon. I am
Too old, and this right hand is grown too stiff
To set the seal upon your later deeds.

ELIZABETH. Will he forsake me who has saved my life?

SHREWSBURY. 'Tis little I have done; I could not save
Your nobler part. Live, Queen! Henceforth you have
Nothing more to fear, need stop at nothing.
Exit.

ELIZABETH, *to the* EARL OF KENT, *who enters.*
Send for the Earl of Leicester.

KENT.   He desires
To be excused. He is embarked for France.

NOTES to *Mary Stuart* ———— Joseph Mellish, an Englishman resident in Jena, was a personal friend of both Goethe and Schiller and is often mentioned in their mutual correspondence. The translation which Schiller commissioned from Mellish before *Mary Stuart* had even been published in German is the basis of the present text. I thought there was something to be gained by the use of the English of 1800 and I knew I couldn't attempt such English myself—except a few words at a time—without courting disaster. As Mellish achieved one of the best versions of Schiller ever made, there was, in any case, no reason not to enlist his services. On the other hand, what even his rendering loses of Schiller's rhythm and glamour makes his script seem long. And seeming long (as against great length *per se*) is a fault. Nor was it to be corrected by ommissions. Even after large cuts were made, the play seemed long. Even short passages from it seemed long! This was due to a manner of saying things which we aptly call long-winded. Everyone took many, many words to get out the simplest thought. It was necessary, not merely to omit certain sentences and speeches, but to compress the sentences and speeches that remained. Necessarily, the task entailed some new writing. The curious are invited to consult Mellish's original effort which was in print throughout most of the nineteenth century.

By offering less of Schiller than Mellish did, I hope to be offering more.

ELIZABETHAN DRAMA
Eight Plays
Edited and with Introductions by
John Gassner and William Green

Boisterous and unrestrained like the age itself, the Elizabethan theatre has long defended its place at the apex of English dramatic history. Shakespeare was but the brightest star in this extraordinary galaxy of playwrights. Led by a group of young playwrights dubbed "the university wits," the Elizabethan popular stage was imbued with a dynamic force never since equalled. The stage boasted a rich and varied repertoire from courtly and romantic comedy to domestic and high tragedy, melodrama, farce, and histories. The Gassner-Green anthology revives the whole range of this universal stage, offering us the unbounded theatrical inventiveness of the age.

Arden of Feversham, **Anonymous**

The Spanish Tragedy, by **Thomas Kyd**

Friar Bacon and Friar Bungay, by **Robert Greene**

Doctor Faustus, by **Christopher Marlowe**

Edward II, by **Christopher Marlowe**

Everyman in His Humour, by **Ben Jonson**

The Shoemaker's Holiday, by **Thomas Dekker**

A Woman Killed with Kindness, by **Thomas Heywood**

paper • ISBN: 1-55783-028-2

CLASSICAL TRAGEDY
GREEK AND ROMAN: Eight Plays

In Authoritative Modern Translations
Accompanied by Critical Essays

Edited by Robert W. Corrigan

AESCHYLUS   **PROMETHEUS BOUND**
translated by David Grene
ORESTEIA
translated by Tony Harrison

SOPHOCLES   **ANTIGONE**
translated by Dudley Fitts
and Robert Fitzgerald
OEDIPUS THE KING
translated by Kenneth Cavander

EURIPIDES   **MEDEA**
translated by Michael Townsend
THE BAKKHAI
translated by Robert Bagg

SENECA   **OEDIPUS**
translated by David Anthony Turner
MEDEA
translated by Frederick Ahl

paper • ISBN: 1-55783-046-0

BEFORE BRECHT
Four German Plays
Edited and Translated by
Eric Bentley

"A breath of fresh air in a mausoleum."

— Herbert Blau

LEONCE AND LENA
Georg Büchner

LA RONDE
Arthur Schnitzler

SPRING'S AWAKENING
Frank Wedekind

THE UNDERPANTS
Carl Sternheim

paper • ISBN: 1-55783-010-X   cloth • ISBN: 1-55783-009-6

CLASSICAL COMEDY
GREEK AND ROMAN: Six Plays
Edited by Robert W. Corrigan

The only book of its kind: for the first time Greek and
Roman masters of comedy meet in this extraordinary
new forum devised and edited by a master scholar of
comedy himself, Robert Corrigan. Corrigan has enlisted
six superb translations to create an unmatched Olympi-
ad of classical comedy.

ARISTOPHANES	**LYSISTRATA** translated by Donald Sutherland **THE BIRDS** translated by Walter Kerr
MENANDER	**THE GROUCH** translated by Sheila D'Atri
PLAUTUS	**THE MENAECHMI** translated by Palmer Bovie **THE HAUNTED HOUSE** translated by Palmer Bovie
TERENCE	**THE SELF-TORMENTOR** translated by Palmer Bovie

paper • ISBN: 0-936839-85-6